C0-AVA-527

ABORTION

CONSCIENCE

#

DEMOCRACY

ABORTION

CONSCIENCE

--- & ---

DEMOCRACY

Foreword by
The Rt. Hon. Joe Clark, PC

Mark R. MacGuigan

HOUNSLOW

Abortion, Conscience and Democracy

Copyright © 1994 by Mark R. MacGuigan

All rights reserved. No part of this publication may be reproduced, stored in a retrieval system, or transmitted in any form or by any means, electronic, mechanical, photocopying, recording, or otherwise (except brief passages for purposes of review) without the prior permission of Hounslow Press. Permission to photocopy should be requested from the Canadian Reprography Collective.

Hounslow Press
A member of the Dundurn Group

Publishers: Kirk Howard & Anthony Hawke
Editor: Nadine Stoikoff
Printer: Webcom

Canadian Cataloguing in Publication Data

MacGuigan, Mark, 1931-
    Abortion, conscience and democracy

Includes bibliographical references and index.
ISBN 0-88882-171-9

1. Abortion - Moral and ethical aspects. 2. Abortion -
Political aspects.   I. Title.
HQ767.M33 1994   363.4'6   C94-931403-X

Publication was assisted by the Canada Council, the Ontario Arts Council, the Book Publishing Industry Development Program of the Department of Canadian Heritage and the Ontario Publishing Centre of the Ontario Ministry of Culture, Tourism and Recreation.

Care has been taken to trace the ownership of copyright material used in this book. The author and the publisher welcome any information enabling them to rectify any references or credit in subsequent editions.

Printed and bound in Canada

Hounslow Press
2181 Queen Street East
Suite 301
Toronto, Canada
M4E 1E5

Hounslow Press
73 Lime Walk
Headington, Oxford
England
OX3 7AD

Hounslow Press
1823 Maryland Avenue
Niagara Falls, N. Y.
U.S.A. 14302-1000

WIDENER UNIVERSITY
WOLFGRAM
LIBRARY
CHESTER, PA

HQ
767.15
.M317
1994

Contents

FOR MY WIFE, PATTY,
AND OUR FIVE CHILDREN,
ELLEN, MARK, TOM, BETH AND BUDDY

FOREWORD

For many people in public life, no issue has been more difficult than the law respecting abortion. It often raises a direct conflict between the pressures of public policy and private conscience, and requires legislators to consider the limits of Parliament's power in a democracy.

Mark MacGuigan and I were colleagues in the House of Commons for twelve years. We were active in different political parties and, naturally, did not agree on every issue. But we were both interested in what governments should do, as well as what they could do. And we both believed that Parliament should not use the Criminal Code to deny Canadian women the option of abortion when confronted with an unwanted pregnancy.

The fashion today is to simplify political issues. Candidates for public office are asked to respond "yes" or "no," "for" or "against," to very complex questions. But even when simple answers are given, they are often the result of difficult, sometimes agonizing, consideration. In this book, Dr. MacGuigan goes beyond simple answers.

As the author says in his introduction, "every politician of national experience instinctively knows that it would be wrong in a democracy such as ours ... to make all abortions illegal." That is less a judgment about abortion than it is a reflection of what we have learned from active participation in the democratic political process. It is an instinct rooted in the knowledge that there are limits to the control which citizens, in a democracy, should accept over their personal lives and decisions. The importance of this book is that it justifies, with careful argument, a position to which many Canadian democrats have come intuitively.

It is not, in the conventional sense, a *political* book. It might be said to be a *legal* book, because it is about what the law should be. It could be described as a history of democracy, since it is replete with historical background on democracy. It might also be termed a book of political philosophy, for it is charged with conviction about the relevance, to contemporary society, of human rights, especially the fundamental right of conscience. But it is most appropriate to call it a work of Christian humanism, which is true both to the best of the Catholic tradition, and to the spirit of democracy.

I think Canadians will find this book timely, probing and persuasive.

Joe Clark

Acknowledgments

No one writes a book as a solo activity: in no human enterprise is it more true that no person is an island. Especially in an extended reflection like this on the implications of democracy for the law of abortion, the ideas of other people are of great assistance. In particular, I have benefited immeasurably over the years from my associations with fellow students and with academic, parliamentary and judicial colleagues. The names that stand out in my mind in this respect are Bora Laskin at the University of Toronto, Francis Leddy at the University of Windsor, and in public life Paul Martin and Pierre Elliott Trudeau.

I am also grateful to the teachers who taught me so much in law, literature, social science, philosophy and intellectual history: Clarence Murphy, Brendan O'Grady, Lily Seaman and G.D. Steel at what is now the University of Prince Edward Island; at the Pontifical Institute of Mediaeval Studies and the University of Toronto, I.T. Eschmann, O.P., Étienne Gilson, John M. Kelly, C.S.B., Laurence E. Lynch, Jacques Maritain (regrettably, only for the occasional series of lectures), Armand Maurer, C.S.B., H.M McLuhan, Anton Pegis, Gerald B. Phelan; R. St. J. Macdonald, Bert MacKinnon, Arthur G. Martin, Desmond Morton and Syd Robins at Osgoode Hall Law School; and at Columbia, Wolfgang Friedmann, Richard N. Gardner, Walter Gellhorn, Harry W. Jones, Michael Sovern, and Herbert Wechsler. Perhaps none of them would feel any kinship with what I have written, but it is a common failing of disciples to take their masters' conclusions as their own starting points.

I am indebted to two friends who have generously read earlier drafts of this work and made many helpful suggestions: Dr. Donald J. McCarthy, Professor of Philosophy, University of Manitoba; and Rev. Dr. Francis G. Morrisey, Professor of Canon Law, Saint Paul University, Ottawa. I did not ask them to agree with what I wrote, but only to help me express it in the most intelligible and cogent way. The imperfections that remain in expression and theory are entirely my own responsibility.

I am also indebted to Dr. Sheila Rothstein for saving me from worse misconceptions of medical science than those I undoubtedly continue to hold.

My wife, Patty, was my most constant source of inspiration and encouragement and also my daily sounding board. In a real sense, this is *our* book.

I owe a great debt to my judicial assistant, Patricia Holland, both for her exceptional accuracy and efficiency and for her unfailing cheerfulness in transcribing not only the original draft of my text but also in making literally hundreds of subsequent revisions. I am also grateful to my law clerk, Faeron Trehearne, for research assistance and for compiling the index.

I am indebted as follows for the right to quote excerpts from copyright material:

L.W. Sumner, *Abortion and Moral Theory*, Copyright © 1981 by Princeton University Press, All Rights Reserved;

Laurence H. Tribe, *Abortion: The Clash of Absolutes*, Copyright © 1992, 1990 by Laurence H. Tribe, All rights reserved, permission to quote granted by W.W. Norton & Company, 500 Fifth Avenue, New York 10110-0017;

Pius XI, *Casti Connubi*, in *Five Great Encyclicals*, Copyright, 1939, by the Missionary Society of St. Paul the Apostle in the State of New York;

E.E.Y. Hales, *The Catholic Church in the Modern World*, Image Books Edition, 1960, Copyright: © 1958 by Doubleday & Company, Inc., All Rights Reserved;

John Paul II, *Centesimus Annus*, © 1991, Éditions Paulines, 250, boul. Saint-François Nord, Sherbrooke, QC, J1E 2B9;

The Documents of Vatican II, Abbott-Gallagher edition, reprinted with permission of America Press, Inc., 106 West 56th Street, New York, N.Y. 10019, © 1966, All Rights Reserved;

Paul VI, *Humanae Vitae*, translation from Appendix One, Janet E. Smith, *Humanae Vitae: A Generation Later*, Copyright © 1991, The Catholic University of America Press, All rights reserved.

Ronald Dworkin, *Life's Dominion: An Argument about Abortion, Euthanasia and Individual Freedom*, Copyright © 1993 by Ronald Dworkin, All rights reserved under International and Pan-American Copyright Conventions, Published in the United States by Alfred A. Knopf, Inc., New York, and simultaneously in Canada by Random House of Canada Limited, Toronto, Distributed by Random House, Inc., New York;

Love Kindness: The Social Teaching of the Canadian Catholic Bishops (1958-1989): A Second Collection, edited by E.F. Sheridan, S.J., © 1991 Éditions Paulines, 250, boul. Saint-François Nord, Sherbrooke, QC, J1E 2B9, Jesuit Centre for Social Faith and Justice, 947 Queen Street East, Toronto, ON, M4M 1J9, All rights reserved for all countries.

Jacques Maritain, *Man and the State*, Copyright 1951 by the University of Chicago, Copyright under the International Copyright Union, All Rights Reserved;

John Paul II, *The Splendor of Truth*, © 1993, Éditions Paulines, 250 boul. Saint-François Nord, Sherbrooke, QC, J1E 2B9.

The Tablet, 1 King Street Cloisters, Clifton Walk, London, England, W6 OQZ, for excerpts from articles by Dominian, 10 November 1984 and 17 November 1984, Moore, 7 October 1989, Häring, 30 June 1990, 24 July 1993 and 23 October 1993, Grisez, 16 October 1993, Lash, 13 November 1993, and from letters by Lash, 13 November 1993 and Fagan, 20 November 1993.

M.R.M.
6 July 1994

INTRODUCTION

I am a practising Catholic. Unlike some fellow Catholics, I accept the Vatican teaching that directly induced abortion is always morally wrong, and that people should be guided by this view in their daily lives. To this extent, my position is entirely orthodox.

However, for me the popular assumption that, if abortion is morally wrong, it ought to be prohibited by the criminal law, is a complete *non sequitur*, one based on a total confusion of the respective domains of morality and law, of sin and crime, in a democracy.[1]

Indeed, I have written this book from the point of view that in a democracy law is not simply morality writ large, backed by the compulsion of the criminal law, but that the two spheres are distinct and separate, each having its own purpose, structure and methods. Although criminal law is admittedly dependent on morality for its legitimacy and acceptance, it nevertheless does not simply incorporate morality — nor morality, law.

In the specific case of abortion, where many people in a pluralistic democracy (in my opinion, it matters not whether they are majority or minority) believe that abortion is not only morally acceptable, but even morally required in conscience in some circumstances, in my view the law may not limit abortion before viability, even if the levers of public power should be held by those morally committed to oppose abortion.

This may seem to some anomalous, since the generally agreed standard for what the criminal law may prohibit is the avoidance of harm to others, and, for many, human fetuses should have the same rights not to be harmed as those already born. (The extent of their humanness — or at least of their moral and legal status — is, of course, often regarded as the nub of the moral disaccord in our society over abortion).

The Wolfenden Report in England in 1957 recommended the legalization of homosexual behaviour between consenting adults in private on the basis that "there must remain a realm of private morality and immorality which is, in brief and crude terms, not the law's business."[2]

As an application of the common good in the field of criminal law, the Report was supported by the Catholic bishops of England, but its principle of the separation of law and morality is often not applied in the case of abortion by the Catholic community north of the Rio Grande. Indeed Daniel Callahan has written:[3]

> The crux of the conservative Catholic legal position is the belief that, in the instance of abortion, it is not legitimate to employ distinctions normally used even by Catholics in other cases involving the relationship of law and morality.

King Baudoin of Belgium, who died in 1993, was regarded as a paradigm of Christian virtue by many pro-life adherents for his refusal in April 1990 to sign a law legalizing abortion. There can be no doubt that, subjectively, he acted morally because he followed his own conscience, to say nothing of his widespread reputation for holiness. But in my view his action was objectively wrong, morally speaking, because it was a failure to live up to his moral obligation in a pluralistic democracy to respect the consciences of those whose moral views were different from his own. He put himself in the same erroneous position as a Catholic legislator who votes against allowing abortion without taking account of the consciences of others. (In King Baudoin's case he escaped the logical consequences of his refusal to sign the abortion law: the bill was deemed to become law without his signature and his abdication was rescinded by parliament two days after it occurred.)

Pope John Paul II has recently raised the questions surrounding abortion and contraception to the level of world controversy at the Cairo Conference on Population and Development. But to my mind, the fundamental issues are essentially the same at the national as at the world level, and are easier to focus on in a national context.

I believe that every politician of national experience instinctively knows that it would be wrong in a democracy such as ours for Catholics and fundamentalists, even if they did constitute a majority in the society, to make all abortions illegal. Governor Mario M. Cuomo, one of the leading Catholic politicians in the United States, has said so many times. In Canada five Catholic Prime Ministers from both traditional parties, Trudeau, Turner and Chrétien of the Liberal Party, and Clark and Mulroney of the Progressive Conservative Party, have either legislated permissive abortion legislation, or accepted a permissive status quo. This is in fact the next-to-unanimous view of Catholic political leadership in both countries.[4] My purpose is to provide a coherent and — I hope — persuasive rationale for this often instinctive position.[5]

In so doing, I shall make use of U.S. experience interchangeably with Canadian in this book, on the theory that American events, social currents and latest thinking have a huge influence on Canadians in this sphere. Although the reverse is not true, there are indications that Americans are becoming increasingly open to the experience of other countries.

Of all active politicians, Governor Cuomo confronted the issue most directly in a 1984 address at Notre Dame University after Archbishop John O'Connor of New York (as he then was) had attacked Democratic vice-presidential candidate Geraldine Ferraro for her pro-choice position, and in my opinion has most fully stated the enlightened Catholic position:[6]

> [T]he Catholic who holds political office in a pluralistic democracy — who is elected to serve Jews and Muslims, atheists and Protestants, as well as Catholics — bears special responsibility. He or she undertakes to help create conditions under which *all* can live with a maximum of dignity and with a reasonable degree of freedom; where everyone who chooses may hold beliefs different from specifically Catholic ones — sometimes contradictory to them; where the laws protect people's right to divorce, to use birth control and even to choose abortion.
>
> In fact, Catholic public officials take an oath to preserve the Constitution that guarantees this freedom. And they do so gladly. Not because they love what others do with their freedom, but because they realize that in guaranteeing freedom for all they guarantee *our* right to pray, to use the sacraments, to refuse birth control devices, to reject abortion, not to divorce and remarry if we believe it to be wrong.
>
> The Catholic public official lives the political truth most Catholics through most of American history have accepted and insisted on: the truth that to assure our freedom we must allow others the same freedom, even if occasionally it produces conduct by them which we would hold to be sinful ...
>
> *I believe that legal interdicting of abortion by either the federal government or the individual states is not a plausible possibility and even if it could be obtained, it wouldn't work. Given present attitudes, it would be "Prohibition" revisited, legislating what couldn't be enforced and in the process creating a disrespect for law in general.*

Not only is abortion permitted by law in both countries, it is so permitted because that is what respect for the consciences of others requires. Indeed, the legal interdiction of abortion is nothing more than a will o' the wisp in a pluralistic society; it is no more enforceable than prohibition. Respect for the legal system as a whole and respect for the consciences of others both leave Catholics no choice but to allow abortion for those whose consciences so dictate.

Indeed, in morals the ultimate principle is not life, as some argue, but conscience, which is closely associated with the virtue of prudence, and by which I mean one's inmost sense of what is right and wrong. Catholics are, of course, dedicated to an ethic of life, but they accept conscience as the ultimate guide to human conduct. As Pope John Paul II recently wrote in his encyclical (i.e., pastoral) letter *Veritatis Splendor* ("The Splendor of Truth"):[7]

> [T]he judgment of conscience ... has an imperative character: man must act in accordance with it. If man acts against this judgment or, in a case where he lacks certainty about the rightness and goodness of a determined act, still performs that act, he stands condemned by his own conscience, *the proximate norm of personal morality.*

Individual conscience can be erroneous, even culpably so. Naturally, people have a moral obligation properly to inform their consciences. God will judge every one of us on whether we have taken the obligation to do so seriously. But, lacking God's knowledge of others' interior states, we must all accept other people's consciences as they themselves represent them, giving them the benefit of the doubt. In other words, if they invoke conscience as the reason for an action, no one can gainsay it, on the basis of a supposedly superior conscience.

In the law as well, the first principle is freedom of moral conscience. Pope John Paul II has written in *Veritatis Splendor* of the "authentic perception" of conscience as the most fundamental of human rights:[8]

> [T]he right to religious freedom and to respect for conscience on its journey towards the truth is increasingly perceived as the foundation of the cumulative rights of the person.
>
> This heightened sense of the dignity of the human person and of his or her uniqueness, and of the respect due to the journey of conscience, certainly represents one of the positive achievements of modern culture.

Since the state lacks the capacity to impose a moral code on its citizens, it does not have the right to second-guess claims of conscience, reducing some to mere matters of personal or social preference or convenience, even if that

might be the best judgment of an objective observer. This lack of state competence was well expressed some decades ago, in a slightly different context, by
Jacques Maritain in *Man and the State*:[9]

> A genuine democracy cannot impose on its citizens or
> demand from them, as a condition of their belonging to the
> city, any philosophy or any religious creed ... [T]he common
> agreement expressed in democratic faith is not of a doctrinal,
> but merely practical nature ... [T]he fact is that the State is
> not equipped to deal with matters of intelligence.

Of course, it would be theoretically possible for a state to maintain a general prohibition against abortion while fulfilling its obligation to conscience
by granting an exemption from the law to those who claimed a conscientious
motivation for abortion. But nothing real would be gained by such a strata-
gem since one can imagine only that whatever claims to abortion were made
would be rested on that basis. There would be a nominal law which applied to
no one.

Therefore, in my opinion, once such a claim is made by any significant
portion of the public, the state must act on it generally, even if some seeking
that liberty may have less-than-conscientious motives, since the state cannot
impose any conscience test on those making such a claim. In such circumstances, a law of general prohibition with provision for conscientious exemption would be an empty shell of legalism, generally discrediting the legal system.

The premise of conscience may perhaps appear harder to sustain in relation to
the American Bill of Rights, where freedom of conscience goes unmentioned,
than in relation to the Canadian Charter of Rights and Freedoms, where conscience is the first freedom guaranteed.

In *Roe* v. *Wade*[10] the United States Supreme Court ruled on abortion in
terms of a three-trimester view of pregnancy: in the first trimester, there is no
role for restrictive legislation — except that an abortion must be carried out
by a licensed physician; in the second trimester, the state may merely regulate
abortion procedures, in ways that are related to maternal health; it is only in
the third trimester that the state may proscribe abortion "except where it is
necessary, in appropriate medical judgment, for the preservation of the life or
health of the mother." The third trimester is the stage following viability, the

point at which the fetus is capable of surviving outside the mother's body. (As I shall subsequently argue, the stage of viability rightly marks a critical point in the legitimacy of governmental control over abortion). Justices O'Connor, Kennedy and Souter, in announcing the opinion of the Court in the later *Casey* case, describe "*Roe*'s central holding" as being that "viability marks the earliest point at which the State's interest in fetal life is constitutionally adequate to justify a legislative ban on nontherapeutic abortions."[11] However, in *Casey* this joint opinion modified *Roe* in relation to the key second trimester by lowering the standard for permissible state legislation from a strict scrutiny approach to one of undue burden.

The U.S. Supreme Court based a pregnant women's right to choose to terminate her pregnancy upon the concept of personal liberty embodied in the Fourteenth Amendment's Due Process Clause, and denominated this a right of personal, marital, familial and sexual privacy. The use of the rubric of privacy, I believe, disguises the essential similarity of this right to that of conscience (which is also the right to make fundamental personal choices — but based on one's view of right and wrong), as well as causing internal difficulties in U.S. constitutional law. Professor Ronald Dworkin has recently suggested a First Amendment basis (free exercise of religion) as an alternative justification of the right to terminate a pregnancy,[12] and such an approach would much better display the role of conscience.

Despite the Canadian Charter's exaltation of the freedom of conscience, it was not adopted as the basis of the majority decision in 1988 in *Regina* v. *Morgentaler (No. 2)*[13] (the Canadian parallel of *Roe* v. *Wade*) for limiting prohibitory legislation on abortion. The narrowest holding, that of Justices Beetz and Estey, concluded only that the then *procedural* requirements of the Canadian Criminal Code for therapeutic abortion did not accord with the principles of fundamental justice in section 7 of the Charter by reason of their delaying access and thereby increasing the risk to health. The similar holding of Chief Justice Dickson and Justice Lamer emphasized as well serious state-imposed psychological stress. Only Justice Wilson in the majority found an infringement of the freedom of conscience, which she felt constrained to introduce through an invocation of section 7 (the right not to be deprived of life, liberty or security of the person except in accordance with fundamental principles of justice). Justices McIntyre and La Forest dissented: they attributed any inefficiency in the administrative scheme to forces external to the statute, particularly to the general demand for abortion.

Personally, I take the view that the freedom of conscience is the most powerful and most fundamental reason for decriminalizing abortion up to the time of viability, but I rest my argument on philosophical principles, rather than on any national system of law. Since I do not argue that the freedom of conscience is the only basis on which the decriminalization of abortion can be sustained, I find no necessity to depreciate the currently governing decisions of *Roe* v. *Wade* and *Regina* v. *Morgentaler*, whatever may be the prevailing winds of jurisprudential analyses of them. These cases contribute their own rationales to a similar end result, even if I prefer a different route.

For me, where matters which negatively impinge on conscience are involved, the criminal law in a pluralistic democracy must follow a "hands-off" approach until viability. By that I mean that, since absolute rights of conscience are involved, the law must impose no coercive burden on conscience, so that no conscience is constrained with respect to those absolute rights. Those who believe abortion to be wrong should be allowed by the law to act on their own beliefs. Those who believe it right should be allowed to act on theirs. The law will thus respect all consciences.

It cannot, unhappily, at the same time respect the moral concern of anti-abortionists who find it excruciating to watch their neighbours take advantage of permissive legislation. That, unfortunately, is the price that democracy exacts when it, before all else, protects conscience from coercion.

It is not intrinsic to my thesis of respect for conscience to argue that the state must necessarily pay for abortions so that those opposed to abortions must indirectly fund them. I do not see such a result as following directly from the principle of freedom of conscience as applied to the criminal law. Nevertheless, in a country with a universal health care plan such as Canada's, this result may be regarded as appropriate for reasons of equality instead of those of conscience.

I realize that, in taking the hands-off position I do on abortion, I run the risk of being seen as a moral relativist by many fellow Catholics. Since I deplore moral relativism equally with them, I deny the charge. What is even more important, however, is that such a charge is entirely irrelevant to what I advocate, because *moral* relativism has to do with morals, not with law. What I do plead guilty to is *legal* relativism. Where diverse people in a democracy hold different beliefs in conscience, the law has no option but to remain neutral in relation to these beliefs, allowing freedom to all, constraining none.

The new papal encyclical letter *Veritatis Splendor*, to which I have already referred, in its comprehensive treatment of papal moral teaching throws no light at all upon the exercise of conscience in democracy. Its central theme is "*the reaffirmation of the universality and immutability of the moral commandments,* particularly those which prohibit always and without exception *intrinsically evil acts.*"[14] It gets no closer to the issue than to counsel that "civil authorities ... never have authority to violate the fundamental and inalienable rights of the human person,"[15] foremost among which, on the Pontiff's own view, is the right of conscience. The problem is not in fact one that traditional morality is adapted to encompass — although, as I have already implied in my comment on King Baudoin of Belgium, on my view of morals, it is immoral, as well as politically wrong, for the state to compel citizens' consciences, prior to viability, by denying them abortions which their consciences dictate.

My own views on these matters have evolved somewhat over the years. I have been consistent throughout my public life in arguing that a Catholic legislator could in good conscience vote for a law decriminalizing abortion, though originally I put that only on the basis of prudential considerations. In an address in 1966, before being elected to the Canadian House of Commons, I said that "a law legalizing abortion [is not] a pure moral issue on which Bishops may instruct the Catholic people on the proper judgment to make, for ... conflicting factual analyses enter in."[16] Consequently, after my election, I was able to take a position in the House, based on my understanding of Catholic moral principles, supporting the 1969 liberalization of the Canadian Criminal Code on abortion (as well as on homosexuality), which was generally inspired by Prime Minister Pierre Elliott Trudeau's view that the state has no place in the bedrooms of the nation, and in the particular case of abortion by his comparison of abortion to self-defence. The bill was brought forward by then Justice Minister John N. Turner, not as representing a "consensus," but only as expressing an "accommodation."[17]

Until the 1969 liberalization of criminal law, the Canadian Criminal Code prohibited abortion entirely, even the therapeutic abortion which was permitted by the law in the United Kingdom. The Omnibus Bill of 1969 allowed abortion when performed in "an accredited or approved hospital" after certification in writing by a "therapeutic abortion committee" consisting of at least three qualified medical practitioners that the continuation of the pregnancy of a woman "would or would be likely to endanger her life or health."

This law was thus an accommodation between various points of view which satisfied none entirely, but it was for the most part tolerable to the public, and it survived for nineteen years, until struck down by the Supreme Court of Canada in the second *Morgentaler* case in 1988,[18] as contrary to section 7 of the Canadian Charter of Rights and Freedoms. But opinions sharpened during these two turbulent decades, and in the aftermath of that judicial decision no further accommodation proved possible, with the end result, to this point at least, that there is no criminal legislation at all governing abortion in Canada.

The Mulroney Government's proposal in Bill C-43, which ultimately lost on a close vote in the Senate and was not reintroduced, might have proved to be the vehicle for a new accommodation, had it not been for the last-ditch opposition of the pro-life supporters. The short two-clause Bill would have required the opinion of only a single medical practitioner that, if an abortion were not induced, "the health or life of a female person would be likely to be threatened," and defined health to include "physical, mental and psychological health."

As I understood the Bill, it would, given current attitudes of medical practitioners, have imposed only a nominal restraint on abortion on demand somewhat akin to that allowed by *Roe* for the first trimester, but it would have asserted a public stake in the issue, by providing for a legislative statement about it. It is somewhat of an irony that it was anti-abortionists, who, one might have supposed, would have preferred even such a nominal limitation on abortion to none, who ensured, by voting with the pro-choice forces to kill the Bill, that there would be no legislation at all for the indefinite future, perhaps forever. Professor F.L. Morton describes what happened this way:[19]

> In the end, the pro-choice and pro-life extremes united to defeat a compromise abortion policy that had the support of the political middle. Canada thus joined, indeed surpassed, the United States as the only Western democracy not to provide at least symbolic support for the unborn child, while still respecting a woman's freedom to choose. Ironically, Canada's new "non-policy" goes even further than Dr. Henry Morgentaler thinks appropriate. Morgentaler believes there is no justification to abort a healthy and non-viable pregnancy after the twenty-fourth week of a pregnancy.

But from the viewpoint of democratic theory, personally I find it preferable that the criminal law remain completely silent on abortion up to viability, the stage of fetal development at which the fetus can exist outside the mother's womb. Such legislative silence avoids the withdrawal of access to abortion by physicians anxious to avoid lawsuits, a result feared by pro-choice groups. Certainly, such an absence of legislation up to viability reflects the ultimate democratic acceptance of diverse moral views. This "no law" position on abortion was put forward originally by Fr. Robert F. Drinan, S.J., a quarter of a century ago, essentially as a lesser-evil argument.[20]

It has been with regard to the diversity of moral conscience that my approach has developed over the years. In my 1969 address on the Omnibus Bill, and generally throughout my time as a parliamentarian, I accepted a decriminalization of abortion for secondary, prudential reasons rather than as a matter of principle, the largest single factor leading to my conclusion being the 1967 statement by then Attorney General Arthur Wishart of Ontario that he would no longer prosecute for hospital abortions.[21]

In the 1969 debate I put my position this way:[22]

> Third — and it is only this consideration which persuades me that some measure of legal reform should take place — there are a large number of abortions now taking place in the hospitals of this country, performed by the best physicians and according to the best canons of medical practice; yet these abortions are all illegal and the practitioners are subject to criminal offences ...
>
> The fact that the law now proscribes all abortions makes for a grave situation when probably at least half the people of Canada believe that abortion is morally right, and when abortion is freely carried out by the majority of the members of the medical profession involved in prenatal care. The difficulty is compounded when the Attorney General of the most populous province is reportedly on record that he will not prosecute violators of this law. When a conviction for an abortion as presently practised in our hospitals is so repugnant to a large number of Canadians that no prosecution takes place, I think we must admit that the law as it stands is completely unenforceable. If we were to allow this legislation to continue, not only would the law be dead in this area but disrespect for the law would be engendered and might go far toward breaking down respect for the law in general. In some part this has already occurred. The public good is not served by allowing this situation to continue.
>
> I therefore reluctantly come to the conclusion that an absolute prohibition of abortion is no longer feasible.

Time was to show that even under the new law, because of the attitudes held by juries, successful prosecutions would be difficult to sustain against medical practitioners like Dr. Morgentaler who refused to accept its limitations.

There were no further issues as to abortion that I was involved with during my elected years, except that I was marginally associated with the *Borowski* case in 1983,[23] where the plaintiff sought a declaration that the therapeutic abortion provision in the Criminal Code was void as violating both the Charter and the Canadian Bill of Rights, essentially because it did not recognize the fetus as a person (an argument based on the word "everyone" in the Charter, "individual" in the Bill). In that case, as minister of justice and attorney general, I instructed the government counsel to take the minimum position consistent with upholding the legislation, and at all accounts to avoid getting entangled in a heavily substantive argument.

In years subsequent, as a judge, I have been sitting on an appellate Court which has no jurisdiction over prosecutions under the Criminal Code, and so I have no occasion to sit on cases involving abortion.

Of course, it could be argued, and was argued by some, that by taking no action over the years I was implicitly endorsing the law and thereby failing to protect the freedom of choice of women. Truthfully, my then cast of mind was that resting in the 1969 accommodation was good law, good politics and good morals. It is in this respect that, with further reflection on the meaning of democracy, my position has progressed.

It is perhaps fair to say that my thinking has evolved in conjunction with much else in society. The years during which Canadian society as a whole, and I with it, remained more or less quiescent in relation to the status quo on abortion were, in other respects, years of significant social change. In the United States, as mentioned, the Supreme Court, basing itself on a newly recognized right to privacy, greatly expanded the right to abortion in *Roe*. In the same period the Women's Movement in the United States and Canada gained enormously in strength and respectability, and focussed its efforts very largely on the cause of freedom of choice. In Canada from the time of the Charter in 1982 on, we had to rethink all of our law in terms of the exigencies of the Charter. As one of the Charter's progenitors, and as a convinced supporter of the necessity of recasting the law in its light, I supported this development wholeheartedly. By 1988, the narrowest basis of the Supreme Court's rejection of the 1969 accommodation did not come as a complete surprise, although it was not generally foreseeable when the Charter came into effect in 1982.[24]

It is now plain to me, as it was not earlier, that democracy requires, as a first principle, respect for conscience. As our society has continued to become more pluralistic, I have personally become more fully aware of the implications of democracy.

It is not that I ever conceived of democracy merely in terms of the will of the majority. In fact, the reason I have been for some forty years a strong proponent of a fundamental charter of rights and freedoms is precisely that I have always seen democracy as a system of government in which majority rule had to be balanced by the protection of minorities.

But the unborn, too, are a minority — and more, a minority without voices of their own to raise in the democratic clamour for recognition. What should the law do about that minority?

As I have already stated, the generally accepted standard now for the intervention of the criminal law is the prevention of harm to others. And if fetuses are accepted as full human beings, they must have the same rights as everyone else not to be harmed; still more, not be put to death. Can they be treated by the law as something less than fully human?

I agree with Professor L.W. Sumner that "the central issue in the problem of abortion is whether the fetus has moral standing ... The liberal's defence of a permissive abortion policy rests on the claim that abortion is a private activity, which rests in turn on denying moral standing to the fetus ... The conservative's defence of a restrictive abortion policy rests on the claim that abortion is (or involves) one sort of homicide, which rests in turn on ascribing full moral standing to the fetus."[25]

I know of no way to resolve this truly horrendous dilemma except by the invocation of first principles. The first and foremost right in a democratic society, I have come to recognize, is that of conscience. By the freedom of conscience I mean, as I have already indicated, the right not to be coerced in one's inmost sense of right and wrong, either by being compelled to do something seen as wrong (an absolute right), or by being prevented from doing something believed to be morally right (a qualified right).[26] In the case of abortion, the breaking point between the two categories is in my opinion the time of viability, the stage of fetal development at which the fetus can survive on its own. Until then, the pregnant woman denied an abortion she conscientiously desired would be compelled to do something she saw as wrong, i.e., continue her pregnancy against her will, and her absolute freedom of conscience would be violated.

However, a woman's absolute right in conscience to abortion is the right not to be compelled to incubate a fetus, not the right to destroy it. Until viability, the two cannot be distinguished because destruction of the fetus is a necessary consequence of a woman's decision not to continue her pregnancy. But once the fetus is viable on its own, it can be only for serious therapeutic reasons, viz., to save the mother's life or health, that its existence can be imperilled. In other words, I would make very much the same distinction as American law in *Roe* v. *Wade*, and will canvass the matter further in chapter 7.

Conscience is an interior right, in fact along with the freedom of thought the only interior right,[27] though of course with external aspects to be canvassed later. I think it is no accident that it is listed first among all rights and freedoms in the Canadian Charter. The freedom of conscience precedes even the freedom of religion, which might be thought of as its exterior form (provided that the freedom of religion is also recognized as the freedom *not* to practise a religion).

Full freedom of conscience can be posited only of human beings who are already born — indeed only, I suppose, of people who have reached the age of reason, or at least that of some degree of moral consciousness — although I shall argue in chapter 7 that after viability, which is a kind of anticipated birth, the life and conscience of the new being must count for something. If the law has to make the truly terrible choice between the consciences of some citizens of full age and the lives of those unborn — since there must be a law one way or the other — it must leave the moral choice until viability entirely to those who are pregnant, for otherwise it would be in the position of constraining their consciences.

Put in physical terms, the point is that the fetus is incubated in the mother, and, until viability, cannot exist independently of her. In the words of Professor Lisa Sowle Cahill in the 1993 John Courtney Murray Forum Lecture:[28]

> What is unique about pregnancy is an unrepeatable combination of factors: The life of one human person is dependent on one other and that other alone; their relation is one of filiation as well as dependency, and support for the dependent being requires habitation of the body of the sustainer.

In the present state of medical knowledge, it is physically impossible for the fetus to survive if removed from the mother's body before viability.

Professor Laurence H. Tribe speculates that the future development of an artificial womb would make it possible to extract, without harm, an embryo from a pregnant women at any stage of development, and that in those circumstances "whatever right a woman might have to choose abortion would be undermined if the fetus could be saved without sacrificing the woman's freedom to end her pregnancy."[29] Such a development would certainly radically change the legal context of abortion. In Professor Tribe's words, "the prospect offers, at least in theory, an end run around the current clash of absolutes,"[30] but its hypothetical nature makes it a matter for the future, if at all. At present, the fetus lives within the mother's body, and any decision of hers to bring her carrying of the fetus to an end before viability has an inevitably fatal consequence for the fetus. Hence a fetus' continuance in existence depends upon a pregnant woman's conscientious decision as to the continuance of her pregnancy. Their sharing of the mother's body leaves the fetus subject to the mother's exercise of conscience. This subjecting of life to conscience is a natural fact, which — because it has to be resolved — has to be resolved by the state in favour of the only conscience in question.

I make no apologies for coming late to this awareness of the fundamental priority of conscience in democratic society. Indeed, I think we should never reproach others — or ourselves — for honest beliefs, honestly expressed. In fact, the evolution of my own position would not have been worth mentioning at all, if my earlier position had not already been on the public record so as to require some justification for a new departure. However, it may perhaps also serve as a case study of the effect of a continually growing understanding of democracy in our society.

꙳

I have complete respect for, though obviously disagreement with, those whose view of democracy and of conscience is different from mine. However, I think that most of my Catholic co-religionists would allow themselves to agree with me if they could resolve two fears.

The first is the fear that, if the right to life is not put in the first place in the democratic canon, then there is no other line of defence against euthanasia as a relatively routine way of disposing of the aged and the infirm. The bishops of Ireland some years ago declaimed of the progress of events in Britain that:[31]

> The delicate tip-toeing into the legalizing of abortion has been succeeded, now that abortion has arrived on a grand scale, by an equally delicate tip-toeing into the field of euthanasia ... Once society accepts legalized abortion, it becomes logically and morally impossible to oppose legalized euthanasia.

The bishops seem to have in mind involuntary euthanasia, where death is invoked against those who have not themselves sought it, but on my thesis there is no logical progression whatsoever from abortion to euthanasia of this kind. Life must yield to conscience in the case of abortion, since otherwise the conscience of the mother would be violated, whereas in the case of involuntary euthanasia the principle of life is opposed, not by some claim of conscience on the part of the person involved, but only by some form of social engineering or social convenience on the part of *other people*. In other words, although the *social* considerations present may be like those in the case of abortion, they are unrelated to the consciences of the terminally ill.

But the present frontier is voluntary rather than involuntary euthanasia (or the presumption of it) where, for example, a terminally ill patient is seeking assistance in committing suicide. The issues in such cases are sometimes more morally marginal, involving such distinctions as those between direct and indirect participation and between ordinary and extraordinary means, and are not easily resolved, whatever the approach. Nonetheless, in the singular case of assisted suicide in terminal cases, I do concede that the principle of conscience could be applied to the same effect as in the case of abortion after viability (i.e., with legislative safeguards), so that aiding in the commission of suicide by a physician would no more be an offence than a physician's participation in the carrying out of an abortion, provided that the act of suicide remained that of the patient, so that the law could ensure that assisted suicide was not used as a cloak for murder. On the other hand, the principle of conscience, as I understand it, would also operate to prevent the discontinuance of ordinary means of treatment in the case of patients in a persistent vegetative state.

The second fear is perhaps even more fundamental. The Primate of Ireland, Cardinal Cahal Daly, recently let the cat out of the bag when he drew from the experience of countries where divorce and abortion have been legalized the lesson that "what is legally permissible rapidly comes to be seen as morally acceptable."[32] I think that in some minds this position is accurately expressed in the companion formulation that morals receives its public verifiability and status from the law, with moral sanctions having the support of criminal penalties.

To me this fear is merely the newest heresy. From morality's being the progenitor of law, it becomes a mere suppliant, beseeching the backing of the all-powerful law so that its own mission will be accomplished. This is substituting the things that are Caesar's for those that are God's with a vengeance. Far from the law's interfering with morality, it becomes a new idol. For the Christian, the First Commandment should dispose of that possibility.

***

What it all comes down to is that there are no easy answers, no quick exits. We have a stubborn problem to which there is no compromise that will please everyone. The positions are irreconcilable, if they are put on the same plane. Only if morality and the law are recognized as on distinct and separate planes is any form of resolution possible.

I believe that we are morally called on as Christians to be democrats as well; that is, to be totally faithful to our own moral principles and at the same time totally respectful of those of others, recognizing that the Christian way is not that of the compulsion and fear of the criminal law, but rather the way of the persuasion and love that has always been the hallmark of the Christian, as well as being the broadway of democracy.

⁂

The rest of this book will be a working out of the rationale of the positions I have, so far, merely sketched.

PART ONE
MORALS

CHAPTER 1

THE MORALITY OF CONTRACEPTION

I f it should seem strange to begin a book on abortion with a chapter on contraception, this oddity has its source in the institutional Church itself, which has improvidently linked these two moral "evils" by associating them in official statements as being apparently on the same moral plane.

More important, the comparison between contraception and abortion will prove to be instructive at the level of law, since the opinion of the Canadian bishops (presented in chapter 4) is that contraception, however wrong it may be thought to be morally, is not a suitable matter for criminal prohibition.

Perhaps most important, in my opinion the only socially and legally viable alternative to abortion in our society is contraception. If contraception is relegated to the same plane of moral opprobrium as abortion, Catholics lose the option of working to reduce abortion through the encouragement of contraception (as well as the fuller provision of societal assistance to those who carry their pregnancies to term).

Turning, then, to the morality of contraception, I may say that I write, not from the theological, but from the philosophical point of view. That should be sufficient, since, according to the papal encyclical *Humanae Vitae* itself, what is at stake is not a matter of divine revelation of a moral principle, but rather one of a natural law accessible to the reasonable mind.

In my view, this papal encyclical letter, issued by Pope Paul VI on July 25, 1968, is the Church's greatest disaster — moral and social — in the twentieth century.[1] Its teaching that each and every marriage act must remain open to the transmission of life is not only in my belief unsustainable,[2] but has been definitely rejected by the leading Catholic theologians and by the Christian faithful around the world. Perhaps its worst effect has been that of prejudicing the reception of official teaching on other issues, particularly on abortion, with which it has been so unfortunately linked by the present pope, John Paul II, who has frequently implied that abortion and contraception are equally grave evils,[3] despite the fact that abortion denies the right to be born, whereas contraception denies the non-existent "right" of a non-existent being to be conceived.

The most analogous ecclesiastical disaster was that of the mean-spirited *Syllabus of Errors*, issued by Pope Pius IX a century earlier (1864), following the seizure of all but a small remnant of the Papal States by Piedmont in 1859–60. Along with exalting the Catholic religion as the sole religion of the state to the exclusion of all others, the *Syllabus* implicitly condemned progress, liberalism and recent civilization.[4] The reaction of the faithful was very similar to that to *Humanae Vitae* a century later. The *Syllabus* was allowed to suffer a lingering untended death in the aftermath of the two World Wars until it was silently interred by the Second Vatican Council in the 1960s.

The 1993 papal encyclical, *Veritatis Splendor,* has proved to be a non-event with respect to the morality of contraception. It does, in a single reference, class any contraceptive practice by which the conjugal act is intentionally rendered infertile as an intrinsically evil act, citing a passage in *Humanae Vitae,*[5] but it adduces no additional arguments for such a conclusion, relying solely on the authority of the *Magisterium* or teaching office of the Church.[6] Press reports that earlier drafts had invoked the notion of infallibility in support of *Humanae Vitae* had created a different expectation, but episcopal pressure allegedly led to the deletion of such passages in the month preceding publication.[7] It remains highly questionable whether infallibility could have been called into such use.[8] In any event, the teaching of *Humanae Vitae* is confined to its own solitary rationale, nothing having been added by *Veritatis Splendor.*

It must be admitted that the overwhelming tradition of Christian theologians stemming from the Fathers and St. Augustine has been condemnatory of contraception, but has at the same time been intertwined with such a host of now reprehensible views that at the conclusion of his monumental study of the subject Professor (now Judge) John T. Noonan, Jr., was led to the conclusion that:[9]

> The recorded statements of Christian doctrine on contraception did not have to be read in a way requiring an absolute prohibition ... The doctrine was formed in a society where slavery, slave concubinage, and inferiority of women were important elements of the environment affecting sexual relations. The education of children was neither universal nor expensive. Underpopulation was a main government concern ...
>
> That intercourse must only be for a procreative purpose, that intercourse in menstruation is mortal sin, that intercourse in pregnancy is forbidden, that intercourse has a nat-

ural position — all these were once common opinions of the theologians and are so no more. Was the commitment to an absolute prohibition of contraception more conscious, more universal, more complete than to these now obsolete rules? These opinions, now superseded, could be regarded as attempts to preserve basic values in the light of the biological data then available and in the context of the challenges then made to the Christian view of man.

Nevertheless, this unfortunate tradition found expression in the denunciation of Pope Pius XI in *Casti Connubii* in 1930, by way of reply to the qualified acceptance of contraception by the Church of England at the Lambeth Conference earlier the same year:[10]

54. But no reason, however grave may be put forward by which anything intrinsically against nature may become conformable to nature and morally good. Since, therefore, the conjugal act is destined primarily by nature for the begetting of children, those who in exercising it deliberately frustrate its natural power and purpose sin against nature and commit a deed which is shameful and intrinsically vicious.

55. Small wonder, therefore, if Holy Writ bears witness that the Divine Majesty regards with greatest detestation this horrible crime and at times has punished it with death. As St. Augustine, notes, "Intercourse even with one's legitimate wife is unlawful and wicked where the conception of the offspring is prevented. Onan, the son of Juda, did this, and the Lord had killed him for it."

One does not need to be a trained Scripture scholar to recognize that the reference to the story of Onan, Gen. 38:8–10, is entirely beside the point. Onan, who "spilt his seed on the ground every time he slept with his brother's wife, to avoid providing a child for his brother," was punished, not for contraception, but for denying his familial responsibility. Indeed, in these more scripturally sophisticated times, it is common ground that there is no biblical foundation for a condemnation of contraception.[11]

Psychologically speaking, what gave the impetus to the reconsideration of contraception during and after Vatican II was undoubtedly the development, by the Catholic Dr. John Rock of Boston and other scientists, of the progesterone pill, which was approved for commercial marketing in the United

States in 1960. But theologically speaking, it was rather a 1951 pronounce-
ment by Pope Pius XII on the natural period of female infertility, in the course
of an address to Italian midwives, that sparked a rethinking:[12]

> Serious reasons often put forward on medical, eugenic, eco-
> nomic and social grounds can exempt from that obligatory
> service for a considerable period of time, even for the entire
> duration of marriage. It follows from this that the use of the
> infertile period can be lawful from the moral point of view
> and, in the circumstances mentioned, it is indeed lawful.

Until that time, it had been thought that not even the use of this naturally
infertile period was acceptable, and this official acceptance of the rhythm
method came to be seen by many theologians as destroying the whole existing
theological position against contraception.

When the Pope removed the issue from Vatican II, in order to allow it to
be considered fully by a Pontifical Commission for the Study of Population,
the Family and Birth, composed of bishops, theologians and lay experts, that
commission voted in 1966, after a three-year study, reportedly by a heavy
majority, to oppose any ban on artificial contraception. At the end, the four-
theologian minority admitted that, in the light of the 1951 statement by Pius
XII, they had no arguments left except that to reverse position would impair
the authority of the Church.[13]

However, the Roman Curia, because of its concern for the appearance of
ecclesiastical authority, found the all-but-unanimous recommendation of the
Commission unacceptable, and a further two-year Curial study led to the
encyclical *Humanae Vitae*.

In the opinion of Fr. Karl Rahner, S.J., "a papal pastoral letter which does
not present any definition [of faith or morals, in the exercise of infallible
teaching power] is basically a teaching which is capable of review."[14] Indeed, it
could not be otherwise, for on any other hypothesis the Church would be forever fixed with the condemnation of Galileo's teaching on the rotation of the
earth, with the mediaeval condemnation of all interest-taking on money
("usury,") with the *Syllabus of Errors* and the "confessional state," to say nothing of the changes in the theology of marriage itself, all of which were issued
in pronouncements of equal gravity.

꿋으ᄋᄋ이

It is common ground to both sides that marital acts have a twofold meaning: as expressions of marital love and as means of procreation. In the crucial paragraphs of *Humanae Vitae*, however, the Curial authors enunciate a fundamentally biological theory of marriage, one which gives priority to the biological principle of procreation, manifested by the insistence that every expression of marital love has also to be a means of procreation:[15]

Respect for the Nature and Finality of the Conjugal Act

11. The conjugal acts by which spouses intimately and chastely unite, and by which human life is transmitted, are, as the recent council reiterated, "good and worthy of human dignity." Conjugal acts do not cease being legitimate if the spouses are aware that they are infertile for reasons not voluntarily caused by them; these acts remain ordained to expressing and strengthening the union of the spouses. Indeed, as experience shows, new life does not arise from every act of conjugal union. God has wisely arranged the natural laws and times of fertility so that successive births are naturally spaced. But the Church, which interprets natural law through its unchanging doctrine, reminds men and women that the teachings based on natural law must be obeyed and teaches that it is necessary that each conjugal act remain ordained in itself to the procreating of human life.

Two Inseparable Aspects: Union and Procreation

12. The doctrine that the Magisterium of the Church has often explained is this: there is an unbreakable connection between the unitive meaning and the procreative meaning, and both are inherent in the conjugal act. This connection was established by God, and Man is not permitted to break it through his own volition.

Therefore, because of its intrinsic nature the conjugal act, which unites husband and wife with the closest of bonds, also makes them capable of bringing forth new life according to the laws written into their very natures as male and female. And if both essential meanings are preserved, that of union and procreation, the conjugal act fully maintains its capacity for true mutual love and its ordination to the highest mission of parenthood, to which Man is called. Men of our time, we think, are especially able to understand that this teaching is in accord with human reason.

Morally Impermissible Methods of Regulating Birth

14. Thus, relying on these first principles of human and Christian doctrine concerning marriage, we must again insist that the direct interruption of the generative process already begun must be totally rejected as a legitimate means of regulating the number of children. Especially to be rejected is direct abortion—even if done for reasons of health ...

It seems to me that this principle of the openness to conception of "each conjugal act" (in the official Vatican translation, "each and every marriage act") is undermined in the very stating of it in paragraph 11. Let us assume, for the sake of argument, that the marital act should be regarded as thus purely biological, with sex intrinsically oriented to procreation. The Curial authors themselves acknowledge that there is not a one-on-one relationship between intercourse (the cause) and conception (the effect). In fact, millions of male spermatozoa may be used up in producing an occasional offspring — or, indeed, with no effect at all. The woman's role is of equal biological importance to the male's, and it has been estimated that female fertility exists for only twenty-four hours in each cycle of twenty-eight days. The relationship between intercourse and conception is thus not a simple causal relationship but rather one of statistics. Hence the comment of Bernard Lonergan, S.J., on contraception that "They'll never prove it's against the natural law for the simple reason that the relationship between coition and conception is statistical."[16]

The relationship between coition and conception is, in fine, one of mere possibility. If this mere possibility is never to be interfered with, then the rhythm method must also be disallowed, because the purpose of its use is to reduce the possibility of conception to zero — even, Pius XII allowed, for the total term of a marriage.

Is artificial conception wrong, "natural" contraception all right, when the purpose is exactly the same in both cases — and, as medical experience has shown, neither method is 100 percent foolproof? How, then, do we justify the use of drugs or prosthetics? How do we justify the use of creams or hair rinses or surgery to offset the effects of aging?

It has never been general Christian teaching that that which just happens in nature is sacrosanct. One of the highest human callings has always been recognized to be the improvement of nature through science and art, to say nothing of the wholesome profession of healing. Nothing could be more typical of human nature than what Rahner has called "the free self-manipulation of man himself — in distinction from animals."[17]

The papal teaching that artificial methods of contraception are in all circumstances and without exception a grave moral offence has been indirectly repudiated by Rome itself. There were persistent reports in the sixties that the Pope had allowed nuns in the Belgian Congo (now Zaire) to use the pill when they were in danger of rape. Now an article with apparent Vatican approval[18] has taken the position that the use of contraceptives by women in Bosnia who anticipate a high probability of rape is licit, on the basis of the principle of self-defence. In this article Fr. Giacomo Perico, S.J., interprets *Humanae Vitae* to apply only to love within marriage, whereas in the case of those threatened with rape "the sexual relations have nothing to do with the act of love between two spouses, in which alone the law of openness to life applies."

To my mind such a position is indefensible. It is of course true that *Humanae Vitae* was dealing with intercourse within marriage, but the requirement that each conjugal act be open to conception, it seems to me, can be defended only on the basis that *every sex act* is rightly oriented to conception.[19] If such a purely biological or physicalist interpretation of the relationship between coition and contraception means anything, what it posits must be true of any mere biological act of sexual intercourse without more. In my opinion the neutral biological act acquires meaning only from a larger human context, not from mere nature. Extraneous relationships like the state of matrimony are irrelevant to nature, which knows no such requirement for conception. If intention is added as a requisite element to the biological act, there is no difference between the intention of a couple using artificial contraception and that of one taking advantage of natural infertility. On the pure biological theory of *Humanae Vitae*, the only relationship which can count is that of coition to procreation, which is biologically identical in marital intercourse, fornication, adultery and rape. On such a theory the personalist understanding of marriage in terms of the love of husband and wife has a decidedly secondary place, and certainly cannot determine the morality of the use of contraceptives.

This failure to rise above biology to human nature itself is ultimately what is wrong with *Humanae Vitae*. The testimony of Professor John Marshall, a member of the Pontifical Commission, speaking of the experiences of the Commission, is deeply illustrative of this point:[20]

Discussion ranged widely over relevant demographic, sociological, medical and psychological evidence but the essential issue which had clearly emerged was not the nature of contraception but the nature of the marital relationship itself. The traditional view of a contract involving "acts apt for generation" was seen to be a totally inadequate description of marriage. Rather, marriage emerged as a relationship of love uniquely, though not solely, expressed through sexual intercourse which may or may not be reproductive.

What is essentially at issue is not the nature of contraception, nor even the nature of sexual intercourse (though that is also very much in question), but, above all, the nature of marriage. This is, unfortunately, an issue on which the Curia in 1968 was not yet fully equipped to speak.

The Augustinian tradition that sexual desire even within marriage is marked by concupiscence resulting from original sin and that the sexual act is always accompanied by sin unless performed solely for the procreation of children was happily not the only current of thought in the history of the Church. But Noonan draws our attention to the horrifying hodge-podge of Christian sexual ethics, which chose early on to follow the guilt-ridden St. Augustine, who saw the marriage act as cruel lust unless performed to procreate (and so not during pregnancy), rather than the more balanced St. John Chrysostom, who approached marriage in terms of spousal love. The Augustinian tradition was considerably tamed by St. Thomas Aquinas in the thirteenth century and St. Alphonsus Ligouri in the eighteenth century. Nevertheless, the first papal recognition I have found of the role of love in marriage was that by Pius XI in *Casti Connubii* in 1930, where he spoke of "the love of husband and wife, which pervades all the duties of married life and holds pride of place in Christian marriage."[21] And again:[22]

24. This mutual inward moulding of husband and wife, this determined effort to perfect each other, can in a very real sense, as the Roman Catechism teaches, be said to be the chief reason and purpose of matrimony, *provided matrimony be looked at not in the restricted sense as instituted for the proper conception and education of the child, but more widely as the blessing of life as a whole and the mutual interchange and sharing thereof.* (emphasis added)

The italicized proviso in this text is of prime importance, because "the very real sense" in which mutual love is said to be the chief reason and purpose of marriage turns out to be a secondary meaning. Marriage as love seems to have amounted to not much more than rhetoric for Pius XI, since for him what marriage is primarily about is the propagation of the species — only secondarily is it about love:[23]

> 59. ... For in matrimony as well as in the use of matrimonial rights there are also secondary ends, such as mutual aid, the cultivating of mutual love, and the quieting of concupiscence which husband and wife are not forbidden to consider so long as they are subordinated to the primary end [of procreation] and so long as the intrinsic nature of the act is preserved.

This grudging acceptance of love in marriage was the official teaching until reformed by Vatican II. In *The Pastoral Constitution on the Church in the Modern World (Gaudium et Spes)* the official Church in Vatican II finally gave voice to a personalist understanding of marriage, which emphasises the central place of conjugal love and a covenant relationship between the marriage partners. The following statements from that document illustrate the revolutionary change in approach which had taken place in 35 years:[24]

> 48. The intimate partnership of married life and love has been established by the Creator and qualified by his laws. It is rooted in the conjugal covenant of irreversible personal consent ...
>
> Thus a man and a woman, who by the marriage covenant of conjugal love "are no longer two, but one flesh" (Mt. 19:6), render mutual help and service to each other through an intimate union of their persons and of their actions. Through this union they experience the meaning of their oneness and attain to it with growing perfection day by day ...
>
> 49. The biblical Word of God several times urges the betrothed and the married to nourish and develop their wedlock by pure conjugal love and undivided affection ...
>
> This love is an eminently human one since it is directed from one person to another through an affection of the will. It involves the good of the whole person. Therefore it can enrich the expressions of body and mind with a unique dignity, enabling these expressions as special ingredients and

> signs of the friendship distinctive of marriage. This love the Lord has judged worthy of special gifts, healing, perfecting and exalting gifts of grace and charity.
>
> Such love, merging the human with the divine, leads the spouses to a free and mutual gift of themselves, a gift proving itself by gentle affection and by deed. Such love pervades the whole of their lives. Indeed, by its generous activity it grows better and grows greater. Therefore it far excels mere erotic inclination, which, selfishly pursued, soon enough fades wretchedly away.
>
> This love is uniquely expressed and perfected through the marital act. The actions within marriage by which the couple are united intimately and chastely are noble and worthy ones. Expressed in a manner which is truly human, these actions signify and promote that mutual self-giving by which spouses enrich each other with a joyful and thankful will.

Not only is this the first relatively adequate statement of marriage in the history of the Church, but it was promulgated only on 7 December 1965, and like other Council documents would have required a generation or two to work through and be absorbed into the life of the Church. But, alas, there was no time! Although the Pontifical Commission, which obviously was on the same wave length as the Council fathers, was able to reflect a similar understanding of marriage in its 1966 report, the fixed mind-set of the Curial authors of *Humanae Vitae* did not allow them the same opportunity for maturation.[25] In the result, we have a 1968 encyclical based on a view of marriage which was decisively — though implicitly — repudiated by the official Church at the end of 1965!

I find myself in complete agreement with Professor Lisa Sowle Cahill that "recent church teaching is moving on a trajectory toward gender equality and toward relationship, not procreation, as the key to sexual meaning."[26] In this trend *Humanae Vitae* represents a backward-looking anomaly tied to an earlier view of the sexual experience in marriage. In Professor Cahill's words:[27]

> It [church teaching] is doggedly attempting, however, to harness these values [gender equality and relationship] to conclusions about sexual morality originally developed out of a view that held women to be inferior, motherhood to be their reason for existence and procreation to be the only full justification for sex. These unconvincing moves damage the Catholic witness on abortion as well as on sexual responsibili-

ty. Instead of showing why commitment and parenthood enhance a sexual relationship, they make these values seem irrelevant to actual sexual experience and oppressive to women.

Those who hold to anachronistic teaching on sexual morality bear a heavy responsibility for the rise of the tendency to relativism in the last twenty-five years among the Catholic population. One might wish for an awareness of this responsibility in the eloquent passages against relativism in *Veritatis Splendor*.

⚜

The reaction of Canada's Catholic bishops to *Humanae Vitae* has been among the most moderate of all national hierarchies. In their first official statement of 27 September 1968, they recognized frankly that "a certain number of Catholics, although admittedly subject to the teaching of the encyclical, find it either extremely difficult or even impossible to make their own all the elements of this doctrine."[28] Consequently, they advised confessors to tolerate the variant consciences of those who could not follow the official teaching:[29]

> In the situation we described earlier in this statement [where some Catholics are unable to accept *Humanae Vitae*] the confessor or counsellor must show sympathetic understanding and reverence for the sincere good faith of those who fail in their effort to accept some point of the encyclical.
> Counsellors may meet others who, accepting the teaching of the Holy Father, find that because of particular circumstances they are involved in what seems to them a clear conflict of duties, e.g. the reconciling of conjugal love and responsible parenthood with the education of children already born or with the health of the mother. In accord with the accepted principles of moral theology, if these persons have tried sincerely but without success to pursue a line of conduct in keeping with the given directives, they may be safely assured that *whoever honestly chooses that course which seems right to him does so in good conscience*. (emphasis added)

This position of the ultimate primacy of conscience seems to be *ad idem* with that emphasized by Fr. Bernhard Häring, C.Ss.R., generally regarded as the leading moral theologian in the Church in the period after Vatican II. In an attempt to break the theological deadlock, Fr. Häring adopted the concept of *epikeia* or equity, a looking for the spirit rather than the letter of a law, as the means of resolution:[30]

> Along with virtually the entire tradition of the Eastern Churches and a large part of the Roman Catholic tradition, St Alphonsus Liguori taught that even in questions of the natural law there is room for *epikeia (Theologia moralis* 1:I:tr.II, c. IV, n. 201). By this he does not of course mean the highest norms of the commandment to love God and one's neighbour that is inscribed in our hearts. Nevertheless he applies the possibility of *epikeia* explicitly to *coitus interruptus,* which at that time was the only non-magical method of birth control, and the cooperation of the wife who knows her husband is going to use this method. Like other moral theologians of that time he too teaches that *coitus interruptus* in itself contradicts the procreative sense of the marriage act and is therefore to be rejected. But he explicitly mentions cases in which couples have good reason to want the marriage act not to lead to conception. He too saw a high value in abstention, but nevertheless left open the possibility of *epikeia* for a just cause (*iusta ex causa*) ... To put it another way, are artificial means of controlling conception worthy of condemnation in all circumstances? The majority of moral theologians side with St Thomas Aquinas in teaching that the more complex and more remote from the supreme principle of love a derived moral norm is, the smaller is its degree of certainty and the less does it exclude the application of *epikeia.*
>
> In the Augustinian tradition the norm of the actual openness of sexual intercourse to creation was an absolute norm, and this was indeed on account of his pessimism with regard to sexuality. For him and his followers the sexual act counted as something degrading and shameful and thus needed to be excused and made moral (*excusatio, cohonestatio*) by the direct intention of procreation. But today one can no longer appeal to this tradition.

But such refinements of moral theology (which in any event justify the refusal of the faithful in their perceived circumstances to follow *Humanae Vitae*) have understandably largely been lost on the laity. Indeed, it can hardly be thought surprising that the laity, which in matters of marriage has a greater instinctive understanding than the clergy, has massively rejected the teaching of *Humanae Vitae*. A recent Canadian poll showed that 91 percent of Canadian Catholics approved the use of contraceptives.[31] A recent survey by the U.S. National Center for Health Statistics indicated that only 4 percent of Catholics in that country follow the Vatican position on contraception.[32] Such results are typical of the Catholic attitude across the world.

Of course, truth in theology is based on the word of God, not on the votes of the public. But all of the faithful are impregnated with the Holy Spirit, and truth in theology is progressively revealed to the Church, through all its members. In the light of Newman's analysis, the assent of the faithful is the ultimate indication that a teaching of the Church has been truly preserved from error by the Holy Spirit.[33] In the words of Fr. Bernhard Häring, C.Ss.R.:[34]

> The Bishop of Rome in union with all the bishops can teach authentically in so far as they are witnesses of the faith of the people of God. This means systemically consulting the faithful, especially those who enjoy a particular experience and professional competence.

What we have is a step-by-step discovery of the truth, not only in the here and now but also in the context of world history. Again in the words of Häring,[35] "Christian theology cannot afford to flee from such historical realities by deriving its precepts only from abstract reflection on biological processes." The ecumenical witness of other major Christian Churches in the West, all of which have accepted contraception, may also count for something, since *Humanae Vitae* is directed to them too.

⚬

In a recent article Bishop Kenneth Untener made use of the analogy of an early map of America vis-à-vis more accurate contemporary maps based on scientific data. When the Pope put aside the findings of his population commission, which urged a change in the teaching, he was seen as clinging to the contours of earlier teachings and reissuing the selfsame map. The bishop states:[36]

> It is hardly a subtle insight to suggest that since *Humanae Vitae*, church teaching authority has been less credible in the eyes of very many people, including Catholics.

If the reason were simply that people turn us off when we preach hard truths, then this is something we must endure. Our task is to preach the gospel in season and out of season, and we must not become alarmed if people don't like what we say.

I believe, however, that there is a different reason for the loss of credibility. Like it or not, justified or unjustified, the fact is many people think that church leaders say one thing publicly and another privately. When we profess our public support for *Humanae Vitae*, or when we engage in "a conspiracy of silence," they feel we lack integrity.

Personally, I would go further than the courageous bishop feels able to in the present climate, where opposition to contraception is taken by Rome as a loyalty test even for the hierarchy itself. The problem is not only the forced dissembling by the hierarchy. It is the overwhelming perception by the laity that Rome's position is devoid of any rational basis. It is in particular contrary to their personal — and personalist — Christian experience of marriage. If the institutional Church can be so wrong about something they (the laity) know a lot about, the laity reason, how can they trust it to be right about things they (the laity) know less about. No amount of thundering about authoritative teaching is going to change that reaction.

The most eloquent statement about the role of sexual intercourse I have come across is one by an English psychiatrist, Dr. Jack Dominian, writing in *The Tablet*:[37]

> For a very long time, and even today, the sexual act was only regarded as properly carried out if semen was deposited inside the vagina so that the procreative purpose could be fulfilled. In other words, the biological component of intercourse was thought to be its chief characteristic. The reality is otherwise. Sexual intercourse is first and foremost an encounter of persons. It is the fulfilment of sexual intimacy at the social, emotional, intellectual, physical and spiritual level. *Personal love and sexual pleasure together form the essence of the sexual act, not the biological potential.* This is how intercourse is experienced by the couple and the attempt to make the procreative element supreme is a violation of its true meaning. Implicitly, the Church has always acknowledged this, giving permission for the sterile and the old to marry, and gradually allowing that intercourse may take place during pregnancy.

Spiritually, the sexual act is the central pivot that sustains the bond of the couple and, as the Scriptures affirm, is analogous to the covenant between God and man and the union between Christ and the Church. In the act of intercourse, the two persons donate the totality of themselves to each other. Male and female, as Genesis states, were created in the image of God for the purpose of sexual intimacy in order to overcome their aloneness and finally to become one. *The means of becoming one in marriage is sexual intercourse, which becomes a recurrent act of prayer of the couple.* (emphasis added)

Dr. Dominian discovers five meanings of the act of sexual intercourse. The first is that of *thanksgiving,* by which the couple donate themselves freely to each other, not as a fulfilment of the other's *right* to sex, but as an acknowledgment of the *privilege* of their mutual commitment. Second, intercourse is an act of *hope* that each will continue to want sex with the other and the union of persons that accompanies it. Third, it brings *reconciliation,* restoring mutual recognition where more than words is necessary for the healing of hurts and quarrels. Fourth, it confirms *sexual identity,* through its encounter of two persons with differentiated characteristics, physically and emotionally. Fifth, it brings *confirmation of personhood,* the complete acceptance of the other's selfhood.

Dr. Dominian concludes:[38]

One of the fears about sexual intercourse which is found in the Christian tradition is that the powerful physical and emotional experience which occurs at the peak of sexual intercourse, and which we call orgasm, is a moment when reason and control are lost. This has been a cause of suspicion and anxiety in the attitude of the Church to intercourse. For a long time, this lack of moderation was identified with brute animal behaviour. That can indeed be an apt description of men and women who desire sexual contact without personal encounter. Sexual attraction detached from the personal does become lust. The supreme challenge which sex presents to the Christian faith is not how to protect its biological component, but how to harmonize instinct with personhood, in and through love.

When personal love exists, the orgasm is not the culmination of uncontrolled lust, but is the fusion of two persons who now become one. Their unity as persons who retain

their individuality mirrors the unity and separateness of the
persons of the Trinity. We should recognize orgasm as the
psychosomatic reality that brings together the physical and
spiritual.

Sexual intercourse, then, is the act which gives life to the
couple on each and every occasion — and, on a few occasions, creates new life. These latter occasions are so few and
the biology which gives rise to them so determined that it
embraces only a minute part of the physiological cycle of the
month. By every criterion, that is to say from the design of
the biological pattern and its physiological meaning, the act
does not remotely require that reproduction should be an
essential characteristic of each and every act of intercourse.
The purpose of each and every act of intercourse is to
enhance the life of the couple.

This personalist understanding of sex and marriage[39] is, I believe, wholly
in accord with Vatican II, as well as with that of the existential experience of
Christian marriage. Procreation and conception thus become secondary —
and, indeed, for the most part, incidental — to the individual act of sexual
intercourse. Where they retain their relevance is in relation to the overall life
of a couple together. It is that whole that "must remain open to the transmission of life," or the Christian concept of marriage will be denied.

Even here, we must remain aware of Pius XII's concession in his 1951
address to the Italian midwives, that the obligation to procreation can be sus-
pended, for sufficient reasons, "even for the entire duration of marriage."
Possibly this is to be thought of in relation to a series of accidental and unfore-
seeable events which might lead to that result. However, in normal circumstances, a marriage of fertile people which by deliberate purpose from beginning to end excluded the possibility of conception in all sexual intercourse
would not be a Christian marriage. There is an inseparability of the unitive
and procreative meanings of marriage in every marriage, not in every marriage
act.[40]

In summation, I think it no exaggeration to say that *Humanae Vitae* is a
dead letter as far as the non-institutional Christian world is concerned. All
indications are that the use of contraceptives by Catholics does not trouble
their consciences at all and that they do not consider it a matter for confes-
sion.

In the context of this book, it is not this refusal by the laity to receive
Humanae Vitae that is important, but the long shadow of scepticism that that
refusal casts over the reception of other teachings on human morality by the

faithful. Indifference to any instruction tends to create indifference to all, and the evidence is strong that this has occurred. In my view, the weakening of the moral resolution of Catholics on abortion is attributable to the institutional Church's lack of credibility on contraception (as well as to its failure to distinguish sharply between the exigencies of morality and those of democracy with respect to abortion).

Perhaps, given this trend, it should be a matter for episcopal satisfaction that only 36 percent of Canadian Catholics find abortion morally acceptable in all circumstances, 41 percent in some circumstances,[41] and that in the United States only 41 percent of American Catholics find the Church's position on abortion too conservative.[42]

I suspect, however, that the reason is more than either good luck or good management, but rather something in the nature of the moral acts in question which is fundamentally different, something which the Vatican, in its hysteria over what it seems to consider the equal sin of contraception, has failed to capitalize on, if not to grasp. The contraceptive mentality[43] into which the Vatican has fallen, by which it seems to attach the main blame for all sexual problems to contraception, has served the Church ill.

CHAPTER 2

THE MORALITY OF ABORTION

Contemporary Catholic teaching on directly induced abortion holds that life must be preserved from the moment of conception, but it does not go so far as to maintain that a fertilized egg is already an individuated human being or person, as does much of the pro-life movement. In other words, the morality is clear: "from the moment of conception life must be guarded with the greatest care."[1] However, various ways of justifying that position are possible, depending on one's understanding of the scientific data.

The strength of the Christian aversion to directly induced abortion from the very beginning of the Christian era undoubtedly stemmed in good part from the fact that the early Christians were faced with a prevalent Greco-Roman code of morality in which both abortion and infanticide were common. Christians reacted in terms of their Judaic and New Testament roots with an ethics of compassion towards all stages of human life.[2]

From the time of St. Thomas Aquinas in the thirteenth century, the Catholic position on the beginning of human life tended to be that which he derived from Aristotle, viz., that a fetus became a human being at the time of animation or ensoulment (i.e., the time at which a human soul was infused, the human soul having been preceded in the same being first by a plant soul and then by an animal soul). Animation was thought to occur about forty days after conception for a male child, after about ninety days for a female one. This attitude seems to have changed during the nineteenth century, and certainly in Pius IX's 1869 Constitution, *Apostolicae Sedis*, it was taught that abortion included the destruction of unformed as well as of ensouled fetuses.

However, the earlier theory of animation affected the development of the common law, which permitted abortion until "quickening," the time at which the mother was first aware of fetal movement, which is usually about sixteen to seventeen weeks. This common law prohibition against abortion became more restrictive in the United Kingdom with Lord Ellenborough's Act in 1803, which made abortion illegal before as well as after quickening. The same prohibition was incorporated into the first Canadian Criminal Code in 1892, and remained the law until 1969.[3] It was also in the nineteenth century that restrictive abortion laws were enacted by many legal jurisdictions in the United States, largely as a result of lobbying by the organized medical profession rather than by churches.[4]

By the time of Pope Pius XI in *Casti Connubii* in 1930, it seemed clear that the Church's condemnation of abortion related to any destruction of the fetus after conception (although there is no direct statement in that encyclical to that effect), and abortion was termed a "very grave crime ... which regards the taking of the life of the offspring hidden in the mother's womb."[5] The Pontiff was most concerned to allow no scope for therapeutic abortion, not even to save the life of the mother:[6]

> 64. ... [H]owever much we may pity the mother whose health and even life is gravely imperiled in the performance of the duty allotted to her by nature, nevertheless what could ever be a sufficient reason for excusing in any way *the direct murder of the innocent?* This is precisely what we are dealing with here. Whether inflicted upon the mother or upon the child, it is against the precept of God and the law of nature: "Thou shalt not kill," The Life of each is equally sacred, and so none has the power, not even the public authority, to destroy it. It is of no use to appeal to the right of taking away life for here it is a question of the innocent, whereas that right has regard only to the guilty; nor is there here question of defense by bloodshed against an unjust aggression (for who would call an innocent child an unjust aggressor?); again there is no question here of what is called the "law of extreme necessity" which could never extend to the direct killing of the innocent. (emphasis added)

Even for Catholics who accept this teaching, this passage leaves a lot of questions without satisfactory answers. Vatican II is of no help in this respect, since its whole treatment of abortion is confined to the following statement:[7]

> 51. ... For God, the Lord of life, has conferred on man the surpassing ministry of safeguarding life — a ministry which must be fulfilled in a manner which is worthy of man. Therefore from the moment of its conception life must be guarded with the greatest care, while abortion and infanticide are unspeakable crimes.

These authoritative documents leave at least three question without satisfactory answers: (1) When does life really begin? (2) Is abortion a form of murder? (3) Is therapeutic abortion ever justifiable to save the life of the mother?

The 1974 Vatican Declaration on Procured Abortion makes it clear that there is neither a unanimous tradition on the moment when the spiritual soul is infused and human life may be said to begin, nor agreement among contemporary theologians. Indeed, this is an area in which theology is very much dependent upon the progress of science.

It is true that all forty-six chromosomes that determine an adult person's separate and distinct genetic identity are present in a fertilized egg or a single-celled zygote (the union of ovum and sperm). But this genetic identity is not yet enough for individuated human status[8] since a single zygote may split at a very early stage into two or more identical zygotes (yielding twins, triplets, quadruplets, etc.) or, very rarely, two zygotes may combine into one. Moreover, before the implantation of the zygote into the wall of the uterus, soon after which (in the third week after conception, the week that follows the first missed menstrual period) it becomes an embryo, there are believed to be a huge number of spontaneous abortions (perhaps half or more of the eggs fail to implant) so that at the earliest stages there may be little permanence of existence.

The attention of Catholic theologians has begun to focus in particular on the pre-embryo stage, the first several weeks after fertilization or conception. During this period it is thought by several that the new life does not have the stable and determinate character necessary for considering it a distinct human being. Several leading Catholic theologians therefore take the position that the zygote or fertilized ovum becomes a person only between fourteen and twenty-four days after conception.[9] The same data lead some non-Catholic scientists to argue that there is no enduring being but only a process.[10]

Unlike in a true process philosophy, however, the argument is not that the process is unending. It stops, clearly, at some point, at least at the point of birth. However, birth would no longer be a reasonable point to take as the end of the process and the beginning of a "being," given the now earlier viability of prematurely born babies. In fact, the evidence of the new techniques of amniocentesis and ultrasound is that a recognizably human individuated being or person exists at a comparatively early stage, before most abortions are performed. Scientific evidence indicates that:[11]

> By the beginning of the second month the unborn child, small as it is, looks distinctly human. Yet, by this time the child's mother is not even aware that she is pregnant. ...

By the end of the seventh week we see a well proportioned small scale baby. (emphasis added) In its seventh week, it bears the familiar external features and all the internal organs of the adult, even though it is less than an inch long and weighs only 1/30th of an ounce. The body has become nicely rounded, padded with muscles and covered by a thin skin. The arms are only as long as printed exclamation marks, and have hands with fingers and thumbs. The slower growing legs have recognizable knees, ankles and toes.

The new body not only exists, it also functions. The brain in configuration is already like the adult brain and sends out impulses that coordinate the function of the other organs. The brain waves have been noted at 43 days. The heart beats sturdily. The stomach produces digestive juices. The liver manufactures blood cells and the kidneys begin to function by extracting uric acid from the child's blood. The muscles of the arms and body can already be set in motion.

After the eighth week no further primordia will form; *everything* is already present that will be found in the full term baby. As one author describes this period: "A human face with eyelids half closed as they are in someone who is about to fall asleep. Hands that soon will begin to grip, feet trying their first gentle kicks."

From this point until adulthood, when full growth is achieved somewhere between 25 and 27 years, the changes in the body will be mainly in dimension and in gradual refinement of the working parts.

To my mind, the conclusion is irresistible from such scientific evidence that, whether or not the earliest phase is most correctly described as a process, at the end of eight weeks there is a being, not just a process: as was said *supra*, "After the eighth week no further primordia will form; *everything* is already present that will be found in the full term baby."

Professor Ronald Dworkin, who has some claim to social observer status as a leading philosopher of the law in two countries, in stating what he calls a paradigm liberal position on abortion, concedes that "from the moment at which the genetic individuality of the fetus is fixed and it has successfully implanted in the womb, normally after about fourteen days ... abortion means the extinction of a human life that has already begun."[12] To the extent that his view is representative, there may not be any sharp debate about whether abortion involves the extinction of human life.

Moreover, the speculations of the Catholic theologians referred to do not contravene official Catholic teaching, which seems to insist only that such new life deserves full protection from the moment of conception, not that it is necessarily fully human at that point. I have already referred to the carefully worded Vatican II Declaration that "from the moment of its conception life must be *guarded with the greatest care.*" (emphasis added) Moreover, the theological analyses of the pre-embryo stage of life are not yet really decisive as to the problem of abortion, since abortion normally occurs much later in pregnancy.

On the second question, despite its use by Pius XI to describe abortion, the word "murder" is to my mind a slogan or emotive name rather than an exact characterization. For one thing, it has more of a legal than a moral connotation, and to the best of my knowledge no modern jurisdiction which has criminalized abortion has ever equated it with murder, or imposed similar penalties. For another, as Fr. Richard A. McCormick, S.J., has put it,[13] "'Murder' is a composite value term that means (morally) unjustified killing of another human person ... To use that term does not clarify an argument if the very issue at stake is justifiability." Besides, on the basis of an assumption of delayed animation, whatever the evil involved in an abortion in the pre-embryo stage, it would not be equivalent to murder in the unlikely event that abortion took place in that stage. I cannot see any justification for a general use of the term "murder," and I prefer more emotionally neutral terms like "killing" or "destruction."

Third, there is the question of the morality of therapeutic abortion to save the life of the mother, for instance, in the case of tubal pregnancy. While accepting the admonition of Pius XI about the direct killing of the fetus, Catholic moral theologians have sharply distinguished such direct killing from indirect killing, where, for instance, a fetus is excised along with part of a fallopian tube, on the basis of the so-called principle of double effect, since what is directly intended is only the excision of the tube for the sake of the mother's health, although indirectly that has the effect of killing the fetus as well. Of such instances where both mother and fetus will die if indirect abortion is not performed, the Belgian bishops in their 1973 pastoral said:[14]

> The moral principle which ought to govern the intervention
> can be formulated as follows: Since two lives are at stake, one
> will, while doing everything possible to save both, attempt to
> save one rather than to allow two to perish.

The use of the principle of double effect in such a case is indeed a generally accepted conclusion of Catholic theology. In fact, Pius XI was undoubtedly referring to such indirect abortions when he added, subsequent to the passage in *Casti Connubii* set out *supra*: "What is asserted in favour of the social and eugenic 'indication' may and must be accepted, provided lawful and upright methods are employed within the proper limits."[15] In the light of this principle, many would take the position that a Catholic view of the law would allow, or even require, therapeutic abortion to preserve the mother's life in these limited circumstances.

The fifty-five Catholic theologians who asserted in a statement on 14 September 1984 that the Church's position on abortion was not monolithic[16] had in mind, I believe, matters of the kind I have just been discussing — the moral necessity to allow indirect abortion to save the life of a mother and the difficulty of establishing the moment when human life is present — as well as the proper political role for Catholics in the abortion controversy. They were predictably, though perhaps not wisely, denounced by members of the American hierarchy, particularly by Archbishop John J. O'Connor of New York.[17]

But although I have emphasized the openness of Catholic theology to the latest scientific findings, many Catholics are persuaded by the scientific evidence that human life begins with fertilization or conception. In fact, that was my own position when I began this study, but my consideration of the scientific evidence has led me to the conclusion that human life begins slightly later (but before abortion takes place).

Fertilization is a sequence of events lasting about twenty-four hours which begins with contact between a sperm and an ovum and ends with the fusion of the nuclei of the sperm and ovum and the intermingling of paternal and maternal chromosomes. When at the end of this short process the nuclei fuse, a new cell is formed, called the zygote.

If development continues, the single-celled zygote divides into two cells, then four, and so on. The first cellular division is called cleavage. There is still only one entity (except in the minority of cases where there are identical twins, etc.) but there is a being of two cells, and eventually of trillions of cells. About seven or eight days after conception, the zygote floats down the fallopian tube and implants itself in the uterus.

It is true that a few entities resulting from the union of sperm and egg are not and never will be human beings. Such are incomplete or degenerated placentas and even rare malignant tumours. In addition, there are all of the fertilized eggs which do not implant and are washed away. It is only with the "hindsight" following implantation that one can be sure that a zygote is in existence, and so not all cases of biological fertilization represent the conception of a new being. But for those that do, it can be argued with some effect that the creative moment has been that of conception. Certainly no other moment in the developmental process approaches in its radical change that moment of the fusion of nuclei of the contributions (sperm and ovum) of the two parents. It clearly marks the beginning of a continuum of life, either immediately human, or quickly leading to human, life. For the zygotes that do not succeed in implanting themselves or otherwise perish, we are unable to account, but there is no necessity to, since, if they ever existed as human beings, they no longer do so, and therefore become irrelevant to the life cycle.

Later moments of significance (but arguably, lesser significance) are the beginning of the heartbeat by the twenty-fifth day and the first functioning of the brain, at about the end of the sixth week, as indicated by the presence of brain waves. Until those moments, the embryo had no need for a heartbeat or an active brain. They are both important moments, but obviously occur to an already living entity, which is not merely a part of its mother's body. It is an entity with a different blood circulation from the mother's, often a different blood type, and often a different sex.

On the relationship of child and mother, Dr. Bernard Nathanson has written:[18]

> [T]he modern science of immunology has shown us that the unborn child is *not* a part of a women's body in the same sense that her kidney or her heart is. Immunologic studies have demonstrated beyond cavil that when a pregnancy implants itself into the wall of the uterus at the eighth day following conception the defense mechanism of the body, principally the white blood cells, sense that this creature now settling down for a lengthy stay is an intruder, an alien, and must be expelled. Therefore an intense immunological attack is mounted on the pregnancy by the white blood cell elements, and through an ingenious and extraordinarily efficient defense system the unborn child succeeds in repelling the attack. In ten per cent or so of cases the defensive system fails and the pregnancy is lost as a spontaneous abortion or miscarriage.

The fetus is thus from the beginning differentiated from the mother, as a different being, even though entirely dependent upon her for sustenance until the stage of viability. Schwarz refers to the biological continuum of the fetus as "a dimension of the personal continuum"[19] and notes that "a previability child is simply one who has a greater need for his natural incubator, his mother's womb, than a postviability child does; just as a fragile, premature baby has a greater need for an artificial incubator than a stronger baby does."[20]

Arguably, the zygote-embryo-fetus is not a *potential* person, but an *actual* person from the beginning. (I am speaking here of persons in a metaphysical sense, not in a legal sense). But even if we grant that it is only a potential person for the first few weeks after conception (which is how I have personally come to see it), it seems to me that that does not change the situation at all in relation to the morality of abortion.

For one thing, whichever of the several possible methods used, abortion does not take place before the seventh week after conception. Heartbeats and brain waves are measurable within the pre-abortion period, and so the fetus would appear to be a human person on any likely test before abortion. More important, even if the fetus were only a potential person at the time of abortion, the abortion would still destroy the whole of that entity's life, the human life-to-be as well as the non-human life already in being. In that case, although it would not be destruction of a human being, it would still terminate the life of an about-to-be human being.

It would certainly be possible in such a case to argue that the destruction of a being evolving towards humanization is less morally wrong than the destruction of an already fully human being, but I cannot see that the difference in moral culpability would be a large one, given the fact that this zygote-embryo-fetus is the only possibility of existence for a human being-to-be. The human person that would have been but for the abortion would now never be. If respect for human life is a part of our moral code, therefore, I do not see how the destruction of such a potential human being could ever be less than seriously wrong, even if it were a lesser fault than the killing of an admittedly human person.

In my opinion, human life has an intrinsic value which begins when the biological life of the human being-to-be begins, whether or not that life is initially human. Such "human" life is often said to be "sacred."[21]

In sum, since I am not concerned to establish that abortion is murder, from my point of view it does not matter whether the entity which is destroyed is fully human or only potentially human. Its destruction is morally wrong in both cases. Nevertheless, the scientific evidence seems to me very strong that the fetus is human before the time at which abortion normally occurs.

I do not concede, as many would have it, that there is no objective basis for judgment in cases of disagreement on morals. Reflection on reality, in this case largely reality as determined by the medical sciences, is what I believe to provide the norms for human behaviour in this area. However, I recognize that many people in our society will not accept my view of the morality of abortion.

Moreover, subjective states of mind are also critically important, particularly in the determination of the correct course of action in a social context. I should have to be unaware of social trends not to observe that at least some of the abortions which occur appear to be based on nothing more than the selfish convenience of the parents. But it is no business of mine either to sit in judgment on particular cases or to estimate the extent to which that is so. What is clear is that there are considerable numbers of people who believe in their own moral consciences that they must themselves have abortions or that abortions must be available for others who conscientiously require them. In the extremes of poverty, deprivation, illness and hopelessness which exist in our world, it is easy to imagine the subjective considerations which lead to such a conclusion. Unwanted children are seen as one of our major social problems, one which, it is reasoned, would be avoided by abortion.

Traditionally, mainstream Protestantism was a strong opponent of abortion. Writing on the traditional Protestant approach to abortion, Fr. Robert F. Drinan, S.J., states that "it can fairly be stated that Protestant theological opinion permits an abortion only for the most serious reasons and does not in any way condone abortion for the mere convenience of the mother."[22] He cites the strongly anti-abortion positions of Karl Barth, Dietrich Bonhöffer, Paul Ramsay, Helmut Thielicke and George Williams.[23] Barth's view is particularly striking:[24]

> The unborn child is from the very first a child. It is still developing and has no independent life. But it is a man and not a thing, not a mere part of the mother's body ... He who destroys germinating life kills a man and thus ventures the monstrous thing of decreeing concerning the life and death of a fellow man, whose life is given in God and, therefore, like his own, belongs to Him.

Drinan comments on Barth:[25]

> It can be disputed whether Barth makes adequate provision in his view on abortion with regard to what Catholic moral teaching would call the principle of double effect, where on rare occasion a pregnancy may be unintentionally and unavoidably terminated if such an eventuality is the

result of means necessary to save the life of the mother.

In the words of the vernacular, Barth is more Catholic than the pope!

However, Professor James M. Gustafson, writing as a Protestant theologian in 1970, reluctantly accepted the morality of abortion in some circumstances:[26]

> As the morally conscientious soldier fighting in a particular war is convinced that life can and ought to be taken "justly" but also "mournfully," so the moralist can be convinced that the life of the defenseless fetus can be taken, less justly but more mournfully.

Since the 1960s and particularly since *Roe* v. *Wade* in 1973, religious opposition to legalizing abortion has been largely confined to fundamentalists and Catholics. Gregory Baum, writing as a Catholic theologian in 1973, had to bring himself to admit that:[27]

> [A]mong the people who regard abortion under certain circumstances as a licit, moral, even if regrettable and extreme form of birth control, are Christian thinkers and in fact several Christian churches. Many Protestant theologians whose work I admire and whose moral judgment I respect look upon abortion under certain circumstances as a moral choice. *In some cases, according to them, it could even be a duty* ... Even when we disagree with the view on abortion, defended by many Protestant thinkers, we must respect it as part of the christian conversation about the meaning of the gospel for modern life. (emphasis added)

Baum goes on to deal with the social context in which religiously minded people may believe in conscience that abortion is necessary, and isolates two factors: the alienation of the underprivileged, particularly the urban dispossessed, and the oppression of women. "The women struggling for their liberation," he writes, "regard any form of unwanted motherhood as an unjust imposition of society."[28]

In contemporary secular thought, moral standing is denied up to the point of viability. As expressed by Professor Sumner, "viability is the earliest time in ontogenesis at which the liberal can concede a right to life to the developing individual."[29] As a legal rather than as a moral standard, this makes a great deal of sense, as I shall develop in chapter 7, since viability marks the point at which the fetus no longer has to live through its mother's body, but can henceforth live through its own.

In my opinion, the movement for women's liberation, which has now became a valid characteristic of our times, goes far to explain why so many people today see legalized abortion as a moral necessity. It is perceived as women's way of escaping from another burden that male-dominated society has imposed; and so, subjectively, is seen as a moral necessity.

Professor Laurence Tribe expresses this point of view strongly in the context of the complete absence in the common-law tradition of a "good Samaritan" duty to sacrifice one's well being to rescue another:[30]

> There is, in fact, only one place in the law where a really significant intimate sacrifice has been required of anyone in order to save another: the law of abortion ... When the law prohibits a woman from freeing herself of the fetus that is inside her, the law appears to work a harsh discrimination against women *even if fetuses count as persons* ... [H]owever voluntary the *sex* may have been the woman was of course, not the sole participant. Yet a ban on abortion imposes truly burdensome duties *only* on women. Such a ban thus places women, by accident of their biology, in a permanently and irreversibly subordinate position to men.

In context it is easy to understand why the right to abortion has become a major goal of the feminist movement.

Unhappily, in the words of Professor Tribe, some "pro-life adherents are quick to denounce those who favour choice as morally blind, deceived by their supposed sophistication into equating licence with liberty and into rationalizing the murder of the helpless as a way to preserve the "quality of life.""[31]

In fact, those who are pro-choice may well be for the most part conscience-led. As Governor Mario M. Cuomo has perceptively pointed out:[32]

> In many cases, the proponents of legal abortion are the very people who have worked with Catholics to realize the goods of social justice set out in the papal encyclicals: the American Lutheran Church, the Central Conference of American Rabbis, the Presbyterian Church in the United States, B'nai B'rith Women, the Women of the Episcopal Church.

Professor Ronald Dworkin sets out a paradigm liberal position on abortion with four characteristics, which he believes to represent the moral convictions of many people in the West. First, since after implantation abortion involves the extinction of a human life, it is always a grave moral decision, and is never morally permissible except for a serious reason. A mother's mere convenience or wanting to have a boy instead of a girl are not sufficient reasons.

Second, abortion is nevertheless morally justifiable to save the life of the mother, and also in cases of rape, incest or severe fetal abnormality. In some cases, he writes, "when the abnormality is very severe and the potential life inevitably a cruelly crippled and short one, the paradigm liberal view holds that abortion is not only morally permitted but *may be morally required*, that it would be wrong knowingly to bring such a child into the world."[33] (emphasis added)

Third, even a mother's concern for her own interests is sufficient justification for abortion if the consequences of childbirth would be permanent and grave for her and her family: for example, if she would have to leave school or give up a chance for a career or a satisfying and independent life. People who take the paradigm liberal view would not condemn a decision to abort as selfish; on the contrary, Dworkin adds, "they might well suppose that the contrary decision would be a serious moral mistake."[34]

The fourth component of the liberal view is that, "at least until late in pregnancy, when a fetus is sufficiently developed to have interests of its own, the state has no business intervening even to prevent morally impermissible abortions, because the question of whether an abortion is justifiable is, ultimately, for the woman who carries the fetus to decide."[35]

I believe that Dworkin has here accurately stated the moral views of a large segment of Western society: casual or convenient abortion is morally wrong, but abortion for a serious reason of health, family or person is seen to be morally justifiable and often as morally required.

Mary Kenny may possibly be right that the knowledge newly gained through fetology in the last twenty years of what transpires during pregnancy will lead to a diminution of abortion, since until now "the convenience of abortion has outweighed regard for the unborn, and when the fetus was unknown it could more easily be ignored."[36] But her prediction that pro-choice supporters will eventually draw back in alarm from abortion may be one for the very long run. Women's liberation, and women's perception of women's liberation, will in my view understandably take at least several generations to be accomplished. In that time the paradigm liberal position will probably change very little.

In the meantime pro-life supporters, of which I count myself one in the moral realm, must recognize that pro-choice supporters are also acting out of genuine moral conviction and zeal. Since society must make allowance for the subjectivity of moral decision making, the clash is one not between the forces of good and those of evil, but between two groups both believing in conscience that their choices are morally right.

It is, as Professor Tribe has written, a clash of absolutes.[37] The collision between the right of a fetus to live and the right of a woman to determine her own fate is not merely a political one. It is a deeply felt opposition of divergent moral consciences.

PART TWO
THE LAW

CHAPTER 3

THE ROLE OF CRIMINAL LAW IN DEMOCRACY

It is common to both church and state to institute rules to govern human behaviour. In both cases these rules of conduct may be referred to as codes when they are written and put together in an organized fashion. Codes which result from religious beliefs are called morals or morality; when they arise merely from custom or convenience they are often termed "mores."

Christianity lays claim to a divinely given moral code, originally as expressed in the Ten Commandments received by Moses, then as refined by Christ Himself in the twofold love of God and of neighbour, and finally as taught by the Church. The importance of moral behaviour was well put by St. James: "Be doers of the word and not hearers only ..."[1] And again:[2]

> What good is it, my brothers, if someone says he has faith but does not have works? Can that faith save him? If a brother or sister has nothing to wear and has no food for the day, and one of you says to them, "Go in peace, keep warm, and eat well," but you do not give them the necessities of the body, what good is it?

The state also has its codes of conduct. They are expressed in criminal and quasi-criminal laws, and in the various fields of law such as torts and contracts which regulate relations among people. In general the interest of the state is in external conduct, although it has to some extent to enquire into states of mind in order to classify conduct. Hence a good many fields of law utilize a "reasonable person" standard, which measures the actual conduct of the parties in question by the way in which a reasonable person would have behaved in the same circumstances. Criminal law alone, because of the severity of the punishments involved, approaches the interior penetration of morality. The mental element (or *mens rea*) required for criminal liability represents an attempt to measure the intention or advertence with which an illegal act has been committed. This is as close as the state can come to sitting in judgment on the rightness or wrongness of what people do. From the Christian point of view it does not reach the moral heart of the matter because it does not — and, indeed, cannot — see into the hearts of the people involved.

Where there are two distinct codes of behaviour, with different commandments, there is always the possibility of conflict. At the very least there is a lack of congruence. That much is obvious, because the codes spring from different legislators, are conceived in different concepts, and are expressed in dissimilar language.

Their relationship can also be seen in different ways according to the disposition of the viewer. In this context it is interesting to compare the attitudes of two members of the House of Lords in different eras. Lord Summer in *Bowman v. Secular Society* in 1917 was very cool to Christianity:[3]

> My Lords, with all respect for the great names of the lawyers who have used it, the phrase "Christianity is part of the law of England" is not really law; it is rhetoric ... One asks what part of our law may Christianity be, and what part of Christianity may it be that is part of our law? Best C.J. once said in *Bird v. Holbrook* (a case of injury by setting a spring-gun): "There is no act which Christianity forbids, that the law will not reach: if it were otherwise, Christianity would not be, as it has always been held to be, part of the law of England"; but this was rhetoric too. Spring-guns, indeed were got rid of, not by Christianity, but by Act of Parliament. "Thou shalt not steal" is part of our law. "Thou shalt not commit adultery" is part of our law, but another part. "Thou shalt love thy neighbour as thyself" is not part of our law at all. Christianity has tolerated chattel slavery; not so the present law of England. Ours is, and always has been, a Christian State. The English family is built on Christian ideas, and if the national religion is not Christian there is none. English law may well be called Christian law, but we apply many of its rules and most of its principles, with equal justice and equally good government, in heathen communities, and its sanctions, even in Courts of conscience, are material and not spiritual.

However, in *Donoghue v. Stevenson* in 1932,[4] Lord Atkin was prepared to base the most fundamental principle of tort law on the tenet of love for neighbour, which Lord Sumner had dismissed as "not part of our law at all":

Acts or omissions which any moral code would censure cannot in a practical world be treated so as to give a right to every person injured by them to demand relief. In this way rules of law arise which limit the range of complainants and the extent of their remedy. The rule that you are to love your neighbour becomes in law, you   must   not   injure   your neighbour; and the lawyer's question, Who is my neighbour? receives a restricted reply. You must take reasonable care to avoid acts or omissions which you can reasonably foresee would be likely to injure your neighbour. Who, then, in law, is my neighbour? The answer seems to be — persons who are so closely and directly affected by my act that I ought reasonably to have them in contemplation as being so affected when I am directing my mind to the acts or omissions which are called in question.

Where there is such a difference in expression, as I have said there can also be conflict. But in the sense in which I understand the word "conflict," that situation exists only where there is a direct collision of commands, either because the state compels the doing of something which is a violation of a believer's conscience, or forbids the doing of something which a believer's conscience requires. For example, until recently many Communist countries formally forbade Christian worship, or effectively discouraged it by strong-arm tactics. An example of legal compulsion in our society may be drawn from the situation of the Jehovah's Witnesses, whose religious aversion to blood transfusions is overridden by the law when the lives of their children are at stake.

Situations of conflict between morals and the law are the exception in democratic countries today. As a rule, when Christian morals and the law cover the same areas, the law provides for a lesser standard than does morality. This is a difference, but is not usually thought of as a conflict, since the law in no way violates the consciences of Christians, who remain free to follow their own higher standard of behaviour.

Perhaps the best example is found in the Catholic law of divorce. By the law of the Church, Catholic Christians may be civilly divorced but may not remarry in the absence of the death of the spouse without an ecclesiastical annulment or dissolution. (Annulments used to be rare, but today, with the admission of psychological evidence as to the states of mind of the parties to the original contract, are much more common.)

The present law of Canada allows divorce after one year of separation in the case of marital breakdown, or with no waiting period where certain forbidden acts have occurred, with no limitation as to remarriage. In other words, the law allows everyone, including Catholics, to remarry after divorce, whereas the Church forbids remarriage unless the civil divorce is accompanied by a Church annulment or dissolution.

This is certainly a difference in perspective, but is it a conflict? Only if we accept the view that one of the roles of the state is to act as a policeman for the Church. The real question, then, is: how is the Church to enforce its laws?

⚜

The Church, as I understand it, and as I believe it understands itself, is a non-coercive society. It attempts to appeal to reason, goodwill and grace. Typically, it no longer indulges in hell-fire and brimstone preaching — though I shall never forget the vivid portrayals of damnation by the Redemptorist Missionaries of my youth! Fundamentally, the Church for the most part is a society of love, not of coercion. That is how I believe it has generally understood its role and mission, and Pope John Paul II has recently emphasized that "in constantly reaffirming the transcendent dignity of the person, the Church's method is always that of respect for freedom."[5]

But in some earlier historical eras, the state (often at the behest of the Church)[6] saw its role as that of the enforcer of Christian morality, because it was thought to be dangerous *to the state* to allow disparate religious and moral views to exist. So, for example, in Spain at the time of the Inquisition, the state dealt harshly with those adjudged by the Church to be heretical. Happily, those centuries have long since passed, and the Church now recognizes its own exclusive responsibility to enforce its laws — not, of course, by force, but by its own methods of proselytizing such as preaching and prayer, which are directed to people's minds and hearts. In this context the greatest penalty will be the exclusion from the sacraments of those who persist in disobedient conduct. The Church, then, does, and must do, its own policing, and in its own spiritual ways.

To put this theory into a more specific context, I would return to my earlier example concerning divorce. The Church will try to prepare its members for marriage by a Christian education, by their exposure to Christian marriage in the parish community, including the example of their parents, and by more direct means, such as marriage preparation courses. Following sacramental marriage, it will encourage prayer, recourse to the sacraments and lifelong fidelity to marital vows. If the marriage nevertheless breaks down, the Church will allow separation and civil divorce, but not remarriage except with annulment or dissolution.

All of this is quite different from the standards of the state, which requires only the fulfilment of certain formalities both for marriage and divorce. But the law is for everyone, Christian and non-Christian alike. It establishes a social minimum, but not a Christian minimum, still less a Christian optimum. Christians understand that the law does not establish their obligations as Christians but only as citizens. They understand that they may be subject to certain ecclesiastical sanctions if they disobey Church law, just as they may be subjected to certain legal sanctions if they fail to observe the law.

Morals and the law are different, each imposing its own obligations and sanctions for disobedience. But they are not in conflict. Christians can — and, indeed, must — meet both standards. They may from time to time find this hard, in the sense that the moral life often involves hard choices. But their difficulty stems from the high standard of their moral code, not from the inconsistency between it and the law. Neither the law nor its minimal standard of behaviour normally creates the slightest difficulty for Christians in their attainment of the moral life.

As I have suggested, the analysis I have just presented has not always been the general understanding of the respective roles of church and state. For many centuries during the age of monarchy, the state took the view that every person in society must profess the same religion as the monarch; variant religions were regarded as subversive and a direct challenge to the authority of the ruler. Gradually there came to be some acceptance of the natural right of human persons to follow their own consciences in matters of belief and religion, but it was only with the American Revolution that for the first time a major nation accepted the legal right of every citizen to freedom of conscience and religion. Put another way, we can say that it was the first time that limits had been set to the absolute power of the state.

But freedom of religion did not come by itself. In the United States it was part of the Bill of Rights, which itself was part of a general constitutional document which provided for the election of those who would have civil authority. In other words, it came as part of a political package known as democracy. It was not, of course, immediately realized. It took a long time for slaves to be freed, and for women and blacks to be given the right to vote. It was almost two centuries before a Catholic was elected president of the United States, and it may be years yet before a Jew, a woman, or an Afro-American is elected to that high office.

≈≈≈

The essence of democracy, as we practise it in the twentieth century, is the rule of the majority, along with respect for the rights of minorities and non-conforming individuals. I might refer to this twofold arrangement as "the democratic compact," because it is not only a matter of constitutional law, but also of an unspoken agreement that the majority will not utilize its numbers to stifle the minority, and that the minority will not use its guaranties to stalemate the majority. There must be give-and-take in a spirit of compromise.

The majority principle extends not only to the election of office-holders, but also to their conduct after election. What it implies is that the views of the majority in a society shall prevail, as to the necessity, the timing and the content of legislation, but not so as to infringe the rights of minorities. Foremost among the rights of minorities to be protected is, of course, the right to freedom of conscience.

That right is not infringed merely by the fact that the state imposes a lower standard in its legislation than is required by the moral precepts of believers. Only a direct violation of Christian conscience would amount to a breach of the compact between the majority and the minority.

Such a direct violation could result from an imposition on Christian behaviour from pro-choice forces, but it could also be caused by the denial of the rights of conscience by pro-life supporters.

Following the *Declaration on Religious Freedom* at the Second Vatican Council, Catholics in most Western countries might have entertained the hope that the democratic compact between church and state and between majority and minority might ease tensions in the future. But, in fact, the hard-won compromise inherent in the democratic compact has been threatened in many countries by the abortion controversy.

CHAPTER 4

CHURCH VIEWS ON THE ROLE OF THE CRIMINAL LAW

The criminal law is the strongest means of enforcing conformity to morals and *mores* which the law possesses. It is precisely for this reason that it is the preferred tool of pro-life forces in the political and legal controversy over abortion that in recent years has become endemic to modern democracy. Recently, particularly in the United States, the rhetoric has become more intemperate as the controversy has gained momentum.

At times the American Catholic Church's position on abortion and criminal law has been outlined in clear but positive tones, as part of a consistent "ethic of life," encompassing also opposition to nuclear war, capital punishment and euthanasia. Thus Cardinal Joseph Bernardin, the Archbishop of Chicago, said in a 1983 address:[1]

> I would ... highlight a basic issue: the need for an attitude or atmosphere in society which is the precondition for sustaining a consistent ethic of life. The development of such an atmosphere has been the primary concern of the "respect life" program of the American bishops. We intend our opposition to abortion and our opposition to nuclear war to be seen as specific applications of this broader attitude.
>
> We have also opposed the death penalty because we do not think its use cultivates an attitude of respect for life in society. The purpose of proposing a consistent ethic of life is to argue that success on any one of the issues threatening life requires a concern for the broader attitude in society about respect for human life ...
>
> The principle [which prohibits the directly intended taking of innocent human life] is at the heart of Catholic teaching on abortion; it is because the fetus is judged to be both human and not an aggressor that the Catholic teaching concludes that direct attack on fetal life is always wrong. That is

also why we insist that legal protection be given to the unborn.

This is firm language, but without any kind of disrespect for those who held opposite views.

This attitude was reinforced by a statement by the American Catholic Bishops in October 1984 on the Church's role in politics. In the course of affirming their positions on abortion and several other issues, the Bishops declared:[2]

> We do not seek the formation of a voting bloc nor do we pre-empt the right and duty of individuals to decide conscientiously whom they will support for public office. Rather, having stated our positions, we encourage members of our own Church and all citizens to examine the positions of candidates on issues and decide who will best contribute to the common good of society ... [W]e are not a one-issue Church ...
>
> On questions such as these, we realize that citizens and public officials may agree with our moral arguments while disagreeing with us and among themselves on the most effective legal and policy remedies. The search for political and public policy solutions to such problems as war and peace and abortion may well be long and difficult, but a prudential judgment that political solutions are not now feasible does not justify failure to undertake the effort.

This is reasonable talk among reasonable people, in which the difficulty of the problem is acknowledged, as well as (and especially) the fact that there may be disagreement on solutions. It is also where the Canadian bishops ended up in 1990.

However, it has been less than clear that the American bishops actually accept their own distinction between law and morals in the unique case of abortion. John F. Kennedy asserted the distinction between the holding of personal moral convictions and the duty of an office-holder. That position was generally taken by American Catholic politicians and was not greatly disputed until the clash of political viewpoints began to focus on abortion after *Roe* v. *Wade*. In the introduction I referred to the conservative Catholic position that abortion was a special case where the normal distinctions do not apply, a "case where the social issues at stake seemed so great that the law had to stand guard over principles at once fundamental to morality and public order."[3] Professor Hans Lotstra states squarely that, although "the American hierarchy ... acknowledge the difference between morality and law," they take the view that "the inviolability of the unborn is a moral imperative of a special kind because the issue touches upon the nature of the State and the very purpose of human law. The State's essential function is the protection by law of the human rights of its citizens; hence, it has the irresistible duty to safeguard their most fundamental right, the right to life."[4]

Moreover, during the 1984 presidential election campaign, Archbishop John O'Connor of New York (as he then was) openly attacked Geraldine Ferraro, the Democratic candidate for the vice-presidency, on the abortion issue, and implied that a Catholic could not in good conscience vote for a pro-choice candidate. It was in part because of the negative fallout from his polemic that the episcopate as a whole had to issue the October 1984 statement quoted above.

However, again in June 1990, Cardinal O'Connor (as he had become), in a statement in his archdiocesan newspaper, warned Catholic politicians who supported abortion legislation, or who favoured providing public funding for abortion, that they were at risk of excommunication, the gravest punishment open to the Church, since it cuts the offending person off from all of the sacraments except penance. He advised politicians "even to accept defeat, should such be the result, rather than sacrifice human life."[5] Earlier, the Archdiocese of New York and several other dioceses had forbidden Catholic politicians supporting abortion from speaking on any subject on church property.

A few Catholic representatives subsequently supported this threat, but the vast majority reacted negatively. Senator Patrick Leahy of Vermont said:[6]

> To say directly or indirectly that on something that is a church teaching that you must vote according to that — that's not acceptable in a country that's based on the First Amendment.

In Canada the Catholic bishops have consistently from the 1960s followed a policy of steady opposition to the legalization of abortion but have not generally indulged in any posturing, threats or imprecations, perhaps because they have from the beginning seen the question of abortion in the context of a wider range of issues involving the use of criminal law.[7]

The responsible attitude of the Canadian Catholic bishops was first exemplified with respect to the legalization of contraception. In a brief presented to a parliamentary committee on 11 October 1966, in relation to the proposed repeal of the then s. 150 of the Canadian Criminal Code, which forbade the sale or distribution of contraceptives and contraceptive information, the Canadian Catholic Conference accepted as a principle the independence of a properly informed Christian legislator:[8]

> The Christian legislator must make his own decisions. The norm of his action as a legislator is not primarily the good of any religious group, but the good of all society. Religious and moral values are certainly of great importance for good government. But these values enter into political decisions only insofar as they affect the common good. Members of Parliament are charged with a temporal task. They may, and often will, vote in line with what the Church forbids or approves because what the Church forbids or approves may be closely connected with the common good. Their standard always lies in this question: Is it for or against the common good?

Hence the only principle binding the legislator is the common good. As the bishops phrased it in a 1984 document, "the purpose and goal of government remains the protection of the common good; i.e., of those social conditions that help each person, families and other groups to achieve their own fulfilment as fully as possible."[9]

But is everything the Church sees as sinful opposed to the common good and so a potential subject of legislation? In the view of the Canadian bishops, sin should be legislated against only if "it be notably contrary to the common good":[10]

> It could be alleged that any genuinely immoral act is at least indirectly and remotely prejudicial to the common good. Yet there has to be a reasonable proportion between wrongdoing and the means taken to suppress it. The comparatively slight harm to the common good that might be caused by certain types of private or hidden delinquency has to be weighed against a much greater potential damage. Clearly, the common good would not be served by a hopeless attempt of public authority to supervise the smallest details of moral behavior through a vast and oppressive network of criminal laws and punishments.

THE FIRST CONDITION, then, for making a moral offence into a legal or criminal offence is that it be notably contrary to the common good. But that is only the first condition. Certain other conditions must also be fulfilled before a law should be passed turning a wrongful act into a statutory crime punishable by law:

1— It should, first of all, be clear, as indicated already, that the wrongful act injures the common good;

2— The law forbidding the wrongful act should be capable of enforcement, because it is not in the interest of the common good to pass a law which cannot be enforced;

3— The law should be equitable in its incidence — i.e., its burden should not fall on one group in society alone;

4— It should not give rise to evils greater than those it was designed to suppress.

Though I find this statement incomplete, as I shall shortly indicate, I am in entire agreement with it as far as it goes.

Applying these principles, the bishops came to the crucial conclusion that the Criminal Code provision against contraception should not be preserved as law:[11]

In the light of these conditions we consider article 150, which forbids giving information about contraceptives as well as the sale or distribution of contraceptives, an inadequate law today. We consider it so, quite independently of the morality or immorality of various methods of birth prevention. We believe it a deficient law because it does not meet all the conditions outlined above.

This has rightly been taken to be a statement of exceptional importance, even though the bishops went on to add that the public in general and juveniles in particular should be protected from uncontrolled advertising for and display of contraceptives, and that the state should avoid campaigning for birth limitation by the public and must always protect from undue pressure the freedom of conscience of those opposed to contraception.

Nevertheless, in my opinion the bishops' interpretation of the common good was not totally complete. A good cannot be common if it is private and personal. Only when it becomes common to members of society can it be called a common good.

Thus in my view, for the sake of completeness, the bishops ought also to have explicitly invoked the principle of the Wolfenden Report in the United Kingdom (presented to the British Parliament in September 1957) that there is an area of private behaviour which is not the law's business. This Wolfenden principle is, in effect, a specification of the common good in relation to the role of criminal law.

The Wolfenden Committee, in recommending the decriminalization of homosexual behaviour between consenting adults in private, took the view that the function of the criminal law "is to preserve public order and decency, to protect the citizen from what is offensive or injurious, and to provide sufficient safeguards against exploitation and corruption of others, particularly those who are specially vulnerable because they are young, weak in body and mind, inexperienced, or in a state of special physical, official or economic dependence."[12] Beyond this area of public morality, the rest is private and beyond the law:[13]

> It is not, in our view, the function of the law to intervene in the private lives of citizens, or to seek to impose any particular pattern of behaviour, further than to carry out the purposes which we have outlined.

It seems clear from a not widely published Report of the Episcopal Committee[14] dated 15 March 1966 that the Canadian bishops deliberately refrained from explicitly embracing the Wolfenden principle, although they noted in passing in this Report that "the Catholic bishops of England have supported the Wolfenden Report, now enacted into British law, which removes from the area of crime private acts of homosexuality between consenting adults." However, the Report states that[15] "there is an area where immoral actions, even those performed in private, have an influence on public morality and so on the common good of society." It would be unfair to focus on the three examples of public-related private behaviour given in this unpublished document, since in any event the Wolfenden Report excludes from the domain of private behaviour conduct that has a public aspect. Taking this into account, it thus appears that the Canadian bishops, like those in England, agree in substance with the Wolfenden principle, even though they could not bring themselves to say so.

In line with their stated position, however, the Canadian bishops' approval of the repeal of the criminal prohibitions on contraception extended also to the repeal of the prohibition on consenting homosexual activity in private, as a 1969 statement by the then Archbishop of Ottawa indicated.[16] It must be said, however, that there was a very disturbing incident in 1986 when the Ontario Conference of Catholic Bishops opposed a legislative amendment to the Ontario Human Rights Code to prohibit discrimination in employment, housing or publicly available services on the ground of sexual orientation, because it apparently believed it was an inappropriate interference with community and moral standards in that it did not distinguish between homosexual orientation and homosexual behaviour.[17] To be sure this was not a matter of criminal sanctions, to which the Wolfenden principle applies, but rather one of benefits conferred by protective law. Nevertheless, the kindest thing to be said about this incident is that the Ontario bishops failed to understand that it was only sexual orientation as such that was being added to the proscribed grounds of discrimination and that offensive conduct (as opposed to orientation) would certainly run afoul of any *bona fide* occupational qualification established by an employer.[18] In my view, the Ontario Catholic Conference displayed a lack of sensitivity on this occasion towards the goal it professed to support of "basic human rights for all members of society including those with homosexual orientation."[19]

With respect to divorce, there was in 1977 a recognition that "no doubt some reform is needed,"[20] but a reluctance completely to abandon the concept of matrimonial fault in favour of the notion of breakdown of the personal relationship in marriage. Both in the 1977 statement and in that of 1985 there was an emphasis on the retention of a court hearing presided over by a judge and on measures to strengthen family life in Canada. In both statements the approach was in terms of the common good, not Catholic doctrine.

As to abortion, the then Archbishop of Toronto predicted in 1968 that the principles behind the bishops' stand on divorce and birth control "would have an entirely different application when applied to the area of abortion."[21]

The strongest expression of what has been a consistently anti-abortion position may have been that in a 1983 statement by the Administrative Board of the Canadian Catholic Conference of Bishops:[22]

[A] law which allows abortion is radically immoral. A Christian cannot accept such law either in its concept nor in its applications.

The document continues with a quotation from the Vatican Declaration on Procured Abortion in 1974:[23]

Nor can a Christian take part in a propaganda campaign favour of such a law, or vote for it.

A 1990 statement is considerably more moderate in phrasing as to the political options:[24]

> During the difficult debate of the last two years around legislative options, some have said that Catholics can support only a law which completely accords with Church teaching. This opinion may have been occasioned by failure to distinguish between the moral law and the civil law or to appreciate the special problems of balancing conflicting claims in a pluralistic society.
>
> While Catholics may not dissent from the Church teaching that abortion is morally wrong, they may differ as to the most effective approach for achieving legal protection of the unborn child. In selecting particular approaches, Catholics are guided by their consciences, informed by Church teaching from which certain general principles can be drawn.
>
> In particular, Catholics may not favour abortion or any proposal which seeks to weaken existing legal protection of the unborn child. Nor may they advocate that there be no legal protection. However, when it is the only available or feasible option, support may be given to legislation which attempts, if only imperfectly, to restore protection or strengthen existing protection and to express publicly their opposition to abortion.
>
> Questions as to feasibility and whether the legislation improves or weakens the legal position of the unborn child, are always matters of prudential judgment where certitude is not possible.
>
> In a country as diversified as ours in matters of religion and ideology, Catholic politicians must assess the legal and political realities they face and work for the law which will provide the maximum possible protection for unborn children.

This analysis shows more understanding of the abortion question in pluralistic democracy than probably any other statement of the institutional Church in our day. It might also be said to provide an object lesson to the more extreme members of the American hierarchy who appear never to have heard of "matters of prudential judgment where certitude is not possible." Until the last few years, it was my own position, and I would have been greatly heartened by its clear episcopal expression. If I venture to depart from it now, in favour of a non-law option until viability, it is for the reason that I have become more fully alive to the profound exigencies of conscience in a democratic society. The bishops are of course right that "genuine pluralism does not relieve you of your necessity to legislate for the common good."[25] But the most obvious difficulty is that there is no agreement in society today over whether abortion is a matter of private or public behaviour. That is the reason that mere invocation of the common good does not resolve the problem.

My analysis of democracy in the next three chapters will, I hope, demonstrate that the first principle of the common good in a democracy is that of conscience, thus introducing a fundamental reorientation to a Christian understanding of democracy.

❧❦❧

In my view the best Christian statements as to the role of the criminal law in relation to abortion have been those of Governor Mario M. Cuomo. I believe he put the issue in proper context when he declared that "the question whether to engage the political system in a struggle to have it adopt certain articles of our belief as part of public morality, is not a matter of doctrine: it is a matter of prudential political judgment."[26] And again:[27]

> I repeat, there is no Church teaching that mandates the
> best political course for making our belief everyone's rule ...
> There is neither an encyclical nor a catechism that spells out
> a political strategy for achieving legislative goals.

What is required in his view is "political realism," not "moral fundamentalism."

Pope John Paul II, in a recent encyclical, *Centesimus Annus*, has provided what might seem to be the basis for a sound approach in denouncing those who claim the right to impose on others their concept of what is right:[28]

> Nor does the Church close her eyes to the danger of
> fanaticism or fundamentalism among those who, in the
> name of an ideology which purports to be scientific or reli-
> gious, claim the right to impose on others their own concept
> of what is true and good. *Christian truth* is not of this kind.
> Since it is not an ideology, the Christian faith does not pre-
> sume to imprison changing socio-political realities in a rigid
> schema, and it recognizes that human life is realized in histo-
> ry in conditions that are diverse and imperfect. Furthermore,

in constantly reaffirming the transcendent dignity of the person, the Church's method is always that of respect for freedom.

This passage might seem to contain a fairly accurate description of those Christians who try to impose their views of abortion on the body politic. The principle of respect for freedom, i.e., conscience, is indeed the very one I urge. However, the Pontiff goes on to say that the right to life, "an integral part of which is the right of the child to develop in the mother's womb from the moment of conception," is "among the most important"[29] of the human rights the state must recognize.

The right to life is, of course, among the most important of human rights, but in contemporary democracy we cannot avoid situations where it comes into conflict with the foremost human right, that of conscience. What is in question, therefore, is not only the Catholic attitude to the role of criminal law but to democracy itself.

CHAPTER 5

DEMOCRACY IN
INTELLECTUAL HISTORY

D emocracy was a late starter in the competition for best form of government, arriving as a historical fact for the first time in a major society only at the end of the eighteenth century.

It was recognized early enough — in the course of the Greek search, both philosophical and practical, for the best constitution. Socrates and Plato saw democracy in a bad light, a viewpoint which was nominally continued by Aristotle. Aristotle's classic statement of the six forms of government[1] is based on the distinction between the One, the Few and the Many, yielding *kingship* (the rule of one in the common interest) or *tyranny* (the perversion of kingship, when government is directed only to the interest of the ruler), *aristocracy* (the rule of many in the common interest) or *oligarchy* (the perversion of aristocracy, when government is directed to the interest of the well-to-do), *polity* (government by the masses with a view to the common interest) or *democracy* (the perversion of polity, when government is directed to the interest of the poorer classes).

In Aristotle, "democracy" was thus nominally a pejorative term. It was government in the interests of one class, albeit the most numerous class. It also had the disadvantage in Greek practice of having officeholders chosen by lot; choice made by vote was considered to be aristocratic, since it involved a selection on the basis of merit — that, at least, was the theory!

From our contemporary point of view, democracy as conceived and practised by the Greeks also had the disadvantage of being limited to citizens, thus excluding women and slaves (much like modern democracy, until recently!). Barker estimates that only about one-quarter of the population of the Athenian city-state fell into the category of citizens.[2]

However, Aristotle himself seemed uneasy with limiting democracy to its nominally pejorative meaning, and was not entirely consistent in that usage. The better manifestation of democracy which he called "polity" he subsequently identified with "mixed government." Polity, he said, may be said to be a mixture of democracy and oligarchy, but "in common usage the name is confined to those mixtures which incline to democracy, and those which incline more to oligarchy are called aristocracies, and not 'polities' — the reason being that culture and breeding [the attributes of aristocracy] are more associated with the wealthier classes [who form the basis of oligarchy]."[3] As a mixture which inclines to democracy, good government by the people as a whole tended to be called democracy, which thus gradually lost its pejorative connotation. In antiquity, however, what we now call democracy was usually called "mixed" government.

The later philosopher Polybius (born c. 200 B.C.), who by reason of being born later had more political history to draw on, perhaps had as much influence as Aristotle on the theoretical development of the mixed constitution (and so on democracy, as we know it). He defined a mixed constitution as a mixture of monarchy, oligarchy and democracy in which each of the three elements has a share in political power and in which none can make use of its powers without being checked by the other two. He found in Sparta (with which Aristotle, too, was familiar) and in early Rome the most perfect examples of mixed constitutions in history.

Kurt Von Fritz gives great credit to Polybius:[4]

> Polybius' theory was taken up, discussed and, with some modifications, adopted by Cicero in his *De re publica*, and though this work is supposed to have been lost until a palimpsest with a large part of it was discovered in 1821, there can hardly be any doubt that St. Thomas had some knowledge of it and was to some extent influenced by it. Machiavelli ... repeats several pages of Polybius' sixth book in a paraphrase sometimes approaching a literal translation without mentioning Polybius' name. From then on the theory in its Polybian form, or in various forms strongly influenced by Polybius either directly or indirectly, remained an important influence in modern European political thought, a development which in a way culminated in Montesquieu's *De l'esprit des lois*.

Nevertheless, at best Polybius' influence worked in the same direction as Aristotle's, and Aristotle is better documented.

Returning therefore to Aristotle, we find that he may be said to have laid the foundation for later constitutionalism in his answer to the question: "Is it more expedient to be ruled by the one best man, or by the best laws?"[5]

> If we call by the name of aristocracy a government vested in a number of persons who are all good men, and by the name of kingship a government vested in a single person, we may say that aristocracy is better for states than kingship ... provided only that a body of men who are all equally good can be actually found.

Nevertheless, Aristotle was somewhat ambiguous on the best form of government. Generally speaking, he favoured the supremacy of law, but he found a place for absolute monarchy (*pambasileia*) "when it happens that the whole of a family, or even a single person, is of merit so outstanding as to surpass that of all the rest."[6] This had the character of a logical necessity rather than of a realistic expectation.

⚜

A similar ambiguity was, moreover, found in St. Thomas Aquinas, Aristotle's first significant Christian commentator, Aristotle's works having been generally lost to the West for a millennium until reintroduced through the Arabs. St. Thomas's high estimation of monarchy may possibly have derived from his respect for divine kingship and for papal rule, though in my opinion[7] his ultimate choice for human government was the mixed form of government, which he describes as a mixture of the other constitutions, in which the law is sanctioned by both the people and those greater in birth.[8]

In a consideration of the law in the Old and New Testaments, St. Thomas advanced a democratic principle as the primary element of good government, viz., that all should have a share in the government (*ut omnes aliquam partem in principatu*), for in this way peace is preserved among the people and all will love and watch over such an arrangement.[9]

The best constitution for Aquinas was therefore one in which one person chosen for his virtue rules over all, with others, equally chosen for their virtue, ruling under him, with a government that belongs to all both because the rulers can be elected from all and because they are elected by all (*talis principatus ad omnes pertinent, tum quia ex omnibus eligi possunt, tum quia etiam ab omnibus eliguntur*). This, said St. Thomas, is an excellent mixture, made up of kingship, aristocracy and democracy.

Even if Aquinas were aware of and influenced by Polybius in addition to Aristotle in this far-reaching analysis, it seems certain that the more preponderant influence was closer at hand in the constitution of the Dominican Order of which he was a member. Sir Ernest Barker has gone so far as to suggest that the Dominican constitution, which was completed in 1221 (several years before the birth of Aquinas), was the inspiration behind the constitutional developments in England in the thirteenth century, through Simon de Montfort.[10] Whether or not this is true (and the evidence, though considerable, is indirect), St. Thomas is known to have been active in the government of his Order,[11] and the close resemblance between the Order's constitution and what St. Thomas lauds for political society is too exact to be merely coincidental. Ives accordingly writes that Aquinas "saw in the government of his own Order a model of a representative democracy."[12]

St. Thomas's fundamental democratic principle foreshadows the words of Article 21(1) of the United Nations' Universal Declaration of Human Rights, viz., "Everyone has the right to take part in the government of his country." There is no textual indication that Aquinas contemplated a periodic change of office holders, with the rulers reverting at the end of their term of office to the status of ordinary citizens, but such a periodic change of leaders and representatives would be in accordance with his Dominican model.

Aquinas' philosophy was handed on in the English tradition, which so influenced the American colonists, principally by the Anglican divine, Bishop Richard Hooker, who restated it against his own Puritan opponents, though focussing more on St. Thomas's natural law than on his theory of government. Hooker, in turn, was a major influence on John Locke, whose *Two Treatises on Civil Government* (1690) became something of a Whig Bible and the philosophical basis of the American Revolution.

Locke considered that the powers of government are limited by the social contract by which men may be presumed to have agreed to live in society. The social contract does not confer on the government any arbitrary absolute power, since the people retain inalienable rights. When government acts contrary to the trust imposed upon it by the social contract, the people have a right to revolt and to establish a new social contract.

On the presumed continuity of natural law/natural rights theory to which I am disposed, A.P. d'Entrèves has pointed out:[13]

> [T]here is not really one tradition of natural law, but many.
> The medieval and the modern conception of natural law are
> two different doctrines.

However, in my own view, the two conceptions are more complementary than different. The later and more subjective natural rights theories took the objective law of nature as a starting point. Natural rights were thought to belong to man as a result of the law of the nature. In the Declaration of Independence, Jefferson based his statement of the self-evident truths that "all men are created equal, that they are endowed by their Creator with certain inalienable Rights, that among those are Life, Liberty and the pursuit of Happiness" on "the Laws of Nature and of Nature's God."

In the world of political reality, it is no exaggeration to say that in Western civilization democracy ceased to exist from pre-Christian times to the establishment of the United States of America. (It might also be argued with considerable justice that real democracy did not exist in the United States until the enfranchisement of women in the first half of the twentieth century and of blacks in the second half of the century.) But in political theory, democracy never ceased to exist, and had a considerable influence as mixed government, an influence that was furthered by the rediscovery of Aristotle. Democracy also existed on a small scale in the mendicant friars (Dominicans and Franciscans). It may also be said that Protestantism as an anti-authoritarian movement marked a step towards democracy in ecclesiastical government, although political democracy was achieved only two and a half centuries later and for different reasons.

⚜

The two striking forms of actual democracy which came into being in the latter part of the eighteenth century, the French and the American, illustrate the two fundamental aspects of democracy, majoritarianism and the protection of minority rights, respectively.

Sir Ernest Barker, Aristotelian scholar and political philosopher of democracy, has described the democratic dynamic as follows:[14]

> That process [of democracy] is, in a word, discussion — discussion of competing ideas, leading to a compromise in which all the ideas are reconciled and which can be accepted by all because it bears the imprint of all.

The axioms of democracy are, therefore, for Barker threefold: agreement to differ, the majority principle and the principle of compromise. According to the crucial third axiom:[15]

> The will of a majority does not prevail when it is merely the formal will of a mathematical majority. It prevails when it has been attained in a spirit, and when it has thus attained a content or substance, which does justice to the whole of the community and satisfies its general and universal character.

This sense of democracy was verified in the United States. Despite the existence of anti-Catholic feeling in the American Colonies and the continuation of state anti-Catholic tests for office in the new United States after independence,[16] by and large, and certainly in the long run, Americans seem to have instinctively understood that majority rule could not extend to oppression of the minority by the majority. In fact, there was no obvious majority, since America was a conglomerate not only of colonies but of different kinds of people. It would not do to substitute the tyranny of the most powerful group for the tyranny of George III. Government had to be limited, not only by the division of powers borrowed from Montesquieu (the theory of checks and balances which he ultimately derived from Polybius), but also by a Bill of Rights to protect the people from government itself.

In the Federalist Papers James Madison expressed the rationale in this way:[17]

> If men were angels, no government would be necessary. If angels were to govern men, neither external nor internal controls on government would be necessary. In framing a government which is to be administered by men over men, the great difficulty lies in this: you must first enable the government to control the governed; and in the next place oblige it to control itself.

Thus perceived as a limitation more on the government than on the citizenry, in the best tradition of checks and balances, the Bill of Rights won general acceptance.

The French Revolution, on the other hand, illustrated rather the tyranny of majoritarianism.[18] The Third Estate, which took over the Estates-General in 1789 and became the National Assembly, was a revolutionary body: though still predominantly Christian in outlook, it nationalized all Church property with no compensation except a salary for the clergy, abolished all religious orders and reduced the number of bishoprics. This Civil Constitution of the Clergy was voted by the Assembly on 12 July 1790, and became the subject of an oath of loyalty for all clergy. Clergy who would not take the oath were deprived of their posts and driven out, imprisoned or exiled, depending upon local conditions.

The new National Assembly elected in 1791 was anti-clerical and even anti-Christian. A new oath of allegiance was forced on the clergy, with nonjurors to be sent to French Guiana if they did not leave France voluntarily. A violent campaign of de-Christianization was then launched in 1792 and 1793 with the clergy facing exile, deportation or death. (Of course, this was also the time of the Reign of Terror and the clergy were far from the only ones suffering). Bishops were forced to abdicate, clergy to marry, images were smashed and churches were closed except when they were seized for irreligious ceremonies.

By 1795 the Reign of Terror and the worst of the ecclesiastical persecution were over. The treaty which ended the Catholic peasants' revolt in La Vendée granted religious toleration to the affected regions and was followed by a general edict of toleration for the country. Nevertheless, until Napoleon's concordat with the Pope in 1801, churches were closed, religious associations, church bells and processions were forbidden, fund-raising was banned, and advertising of the Mass was not allowed. Even a century later, every time revolutionary fervour grew and revolutionaries were in government, persecution of Christianity flourished.

I have emphasized persecution of the Church, not because it was the only excess of the revolutionaries — far from it! — but because the anti-Christian fever seemed to be the most primitive as well as the most ideological expression of the revolutionary virus.

Edmund Burke, watching closely from England, foresaw from the beginning in his *Reflections on the Revolution in France* in 1790 not only the terror and the massacres that would subsequently take place with an intensification of the Revolution, but of which there was as then no sign, but also the military despotism which would eventually replace it. Burke, who had been the strongest English supporter of the American Revolution, became the strongest foe of the French, primarily because of its anti-religious venom and its generally illiberal and, indeed, totalitarian character.[19]

Throughout the nineteenth century it was the still vivid memory of the French Revolution which, depending on one's point of view, either inspired or repelled. However, particularly with the new status of the United States after the two World Wars as, first, one of two superpowers, and, now, the only superpower, it is the American democratic experiment and experience that has come to dominate the attention of the whole world.

Constitutionalism, by which I mean the limitation of government absolutism through constitutional protections, has been gradually gaining the day around the globe. Bills of rights have been proliferating in states old and new. Even non-democratic states feel the need to claim to be democratic because only democracy is seen as respectable.

The age of democracy has arrived in the world, and, happily, that democracy is the kind that exalts not *vox populi* alone, but combines majoritarianism with the protection of human rights. The mixed government of the ancients has become the democracy of today.

CHAPTER 6

THE CHURCH AND DEMOCRACY

The necessary distinction between the "things" of God and those of Caesar is as old as Christianity itself. It assumed institutional form for the Christian with the recognition of Christianity as the official religion of Rome by Constantine the Great in the first part of the fourth century. From that time on the tension between the spiritual power and the temporal power, the sacral and the profane, church and state, was one of the constants of existence.

That tension was exacerbated in the long run by the gift of the Papal States to the popes by the Carolingian kings of the eighth century. In the short run, the gift no doubt achieved its purpose of protecting the popes from the tyranny of factions and princes. It certainly was not the principal cause of much of the tension between popes and kings or emperors. Popes Innocent III and Boniface VIII, for instance, asserted their papal prerogatives not as temporal rulers but as spiritual ones. But already, by the Renaissance, the Carolingian donation was (in retrospect at least) an embarrassment, entangling the papacy in the petty squabbles of Italian politics. Indeed, it was only because Italy was somewhat of a political backwater during the second half of the sixteenth century, as well as during the seventeenth and eighteenth centuries, and because in any event the popes of the Catholic Reformation took a larger-than-parochial view of their mission, that the troublemaking potential of the Papal States was not earlier realized. However, during the nearly century and a half between the French Revolution in 1789 and the Lateran Treaty between Pope Pius XI and Mussolini in 1929, when the pope's temporal status was finally resolved by the creation of the tiny Vatican City state, the Papal States were a continual magnet for avaricious powers, as well as a distraction from higher responsibilities for the popes. Incidentally (and perhaps ironically, after many centuries of friction), E.E.Y. Hales notes that the present-day Vatican state "corresponds closely, in area, with the Leonine State of the fifth century, before the Carolingian accretions."[1]

The existence of the Papal States had a particularly unfortunate role in the Church's coming to terms with the rise of political democracy. For one thing, the popes were for the most part benevolent but also paternalistic and inefficient temporal rulers. Hales notes that:[2]

> [I]n its adminstration and in its legal machinery, the papal regime was out of date; it may have been a paternal theocracy, it may have been more merciful than the general run of petty despotism in Germany or Italy at that time [of Pius IX], but politically and economically it was behind the times.

The absence of compromise with Piedmont, the northern Italian state of Victor Emmanuel and Cavour, Mazzini and Garibaldi, which eventually united all Italy, was by no means all the fault of Pio Nono. Piedmont was in the hands of persecution-minded secularist zealots who showed within their own state how far they were prepared to go in suppressing Catholicism. But the Pope's determination to defend his territorial patrimony, even to the extent of establishing an army through international recruiting in 1859, condemned the Church to a treadmill of political conflict that lasted for generations.

At the bottom was the reluctance, not only of the popes, but also of most Catholics in Europe, to come to grips with the French Revolution of 1789 and the liberal democracy which gradually emerged from the revolutionary chaos. The loss of all the Papal States by 1860, except for a narrow strip of land along the western coast of Italy (including Rome), was one of the major underlying causes of the disaster of the *Syllabus of Errors* in 1864. (The remaining papal territory was subsequently absorbed by Italy in 1870, and in 1871 Rome was proclaimed the capital of the Kingdom of Italy.)

The nineteenth-century popes were to some extent favourably impressed by the advantages to the Church of the separation of church and state that obtained in the United States of America. There, the pope could make his episcopal appointments as he chose, without the agreement of the government, his orders could be published without permission, and he could create dioceses, seminaries and colleges as deemed fit without authorization, whereas no European government except that of the United Kingdom allowed the Church similar freedom. In fact, liberal Catholics in Europe like Lamennais and his followers were urging precisely the same kind of church-state relationship in Europe as existed in the United States, but earned denunciation for their pains.

The problem with the American model from the popes' point of view was, first, with the European governments. Even Catholic monarchs displayed time and again their determination to interfere in the internal affairs of the

Church. Behind them, and often succeeding them (as in France after the Franco-Prussian War) were aggressive secularists of the most extreme kind, determined to strip every vestige, not only of the Church, but of Christianity, from their societies.[3]

Second, the popes had a serious problem with the conservative, usually pro-monarchist, views of the Catholic people. The virulence of the anti-religious coterie in government was sparked in part by the stubborn resistance of Catholics generally to democracy, and in France to republicanism. The popes had constantly to strive to moderate the political attitudes of the faithful.[4]

Third, there was some suspicion on the part of European Catholics of what was sometimes called the "American heresy," which in 1899 led Pope Leo XIII to address his letter *Testem Benevolentiae* to Cardinal Gibbons, the archbishop of Baltimore from 1877 to 1921. "Americanism" may well have been a figment of the European imagination. At most, it stood for a way of life which was too likely to lead to accommodation, secularism and indifferentism. In the words of Hales, "as Leo XIII himself said, the condemnation was needed rather to clarify opinion in France than opinion in America."[5]

Finally, it must be frankly admitted that the separation of church and state, as it existed in the United States, was not perceived by the official Church of that time as the ideal relationship. The ideal was still an "established" Church, with the state officially committed to the propagation of the faith. This ideal has often been referred to as the "confessional state," a state which confesses or formally avows the truth of the Catholic religion. The most celebrated twentieth-century opponent of this church-state theory, Fr. John Courtney Murray, S.J., referred to it as the Church's dealing with the secular order "in terms of a double standard — freedom for the Church when Catholics are in a minority, privilege for the Church and intolerance for others when Catholics are a majority."[6]

This reactionary attitude on the part of the popes, and probably of most European Catholics, was in sharp contrast with that of the minority of liberal Catholics in nineteenth-century Europe. As early as the 1820s, Lamennais in France, although as a strong ultramontane a supporter of papal power over civil government, urged the Church to rely on the people rather than governments, supporting democratic and revolutionary movements. True religion for him could exist only in "a free Church in a free State." His views were condemned by Pope Gregory XVI in the encyclical *Mirari Vos* in 1832. The Pope took the view, in the words of Hales, that:[7]

> State indifference in matters of religion was a "perverse view";
> liberty of conscience (by which Lamennais meant liberty for

everybody to pick and choose between religions) was an "absurd or rather ludicrous maxim"; liberty of the press was "execrable"; separation of Church and State was a "dream."

Lamennais eventually left the Church, but his struggle was carried on within the Church by Montalembert, Lacordaire, Bishop Dupanloup, Döllinger, and Lord Acton.

For Acton, in John Nurser's words, "the American Revolution was the turning point of world history":[8]

> His Cambridge *Lectures on Modern History*, the shape of his mature thought, begin with the formulation of a political idea of conscience in Aquinas, and conclude with the achieved majesty of the Federal Liberal State in America.

He followed Edmund Burke in seeing the pathology of the French Revolution, whereas the fundamental element of the American Revolution for him was its vision of the natural rights of people as people.

It was not that Americans were free of religious prejudice. In the words of Conor Cruise O'Brien, at the Revolutionary Period "America ... was more anti-Catholic than Britain. And the revolutionaries exploited and fanned anti-Catholicism, especially in the pulpits of New England, for their own political purpose."[9] The Continental Congress' 1774 "Address to the People of Great Britain," following the Québec Act, denounced the establishment in Canada of a "religion that has deluged your island in blood and disbursed impurity, bigotry, persecution, murder and rebellion through every part of the world."[10] The violent anti-Catholicism of the Know-Nothings continued the same spirit half a century later, and Judge John T. Noonan, Jr., has pointed out that "religious establishments lasted as late as 1870."[11]

It was not affection for Catholics that led to the forbidding of religious tests for federal office in Article VI of the U.S. Constitution or to the First Amendment provision that "Congress shall make no law respecting an establishment of religion or prohibiting the free exercise thereof ..." It was rather that a permanent political union between people of such diverse religious groups as Congregationalists and Episcopalians was not possible on any other basis. The religiously neutral state was created more by political necessity than out of any spirit of religious toleration, but once established, its philosophical adumbration followed.

For Acton the fundamental notion in political theory was that of conscience. Through it, every person has access to the common source of morality.

Liberty is nothing more than the "Reign of Conscience," with "Reason commanding reason, not will commanding will," with consequent "Safety of minorities."[12] Nurser writes:[13]

> Acton repeatedly quotes Hamilton's famous saying that the
> principles of political justice are "written on the conscience
> of mankind by the finger of God." In the American
> Revolution, Acton believed, the national sense of justice had
> expressed what was universal natural law.

The total separation of church and state was for Acton the guarantee of conscience: the church is a check on the state, and the state on the church. The separation is beneficial to both. As was said above, in Acton "liberty" is nothing more than "the Reign of Conscience." Conscience is "the political absolute" and America "its home."[14] For Acton, liberty was born in the United States, because, for the first time in history, conscience, "the voice of God" was given full scope vis-à-vis authority, which is "the voice of man."[15]

In the twentieth century the leading figure in Catholic intellectual history in relation to church and state has been the great French philosopher Jacques Maritain. Like Acton, he considered the U.S. Constitution a landmark of human achievement:[16]

> Peerless is the significance, for political philosophy, of the
> establishment of the American Constitution at the end of the
> XVIIIth Century. This Constitution can be described as an
> outstanding lay Christian document tinged with the philoso-
> phy of the day.

For Maritain, the sacral era of the Middle Ages, in which an attempt was made to build civilization on the unity of religious faith, must be put behind us as forever past. Indeed, the leavening influence of the Gospel has itself brought about the more perfect state of affairs in which the common good of a pluralist society becomes the basis of political life:[17]

> In proportion as the civil society has become now perfectly
> distinguished from the spiritual realm of the Church — a
> process which was in itself but a development of the Gospel

distinction between the things that are Caesar's and the things that are God's — the civil society has become grounded on a common good and a common task which are of an earthly, "temporal" or "secular" order, and in which citizens belonging to diverse spiritual groups or lineages share equally. Religious division among men is in itself a misfortune. But it is a fact that we must willy-nilly recognize.

It is, to my mind, hard to exaggerate the importance of this Maritainian recognition of a religiously neutral, pluralist democracy as a higher stage in the evolution of divine providence for the world, a development of the Gospel distinction between the Two Powers which has led to a civil common good "in which citizens belonging to diverse spiritual groups or lineages share equally." This is more than a mere toleration of diversity. It is an acceptance of pluralistic society as God's plan for the world.

Maritain's theories show how Catholic thought was definitely progressing in its acceptance of democracy, even though official teaching had not gone beyond the *Syllabus of Errors*. Indeed, in my opinion, by the end of the Second World War virtually every Catholic lay person in the Western world instinctively understood that political democracy, not the confessional state, was the form of government most compatible with the Catholic faith.

No one suffered more from the discrepancy between the old official position and the new realization that all lay Catholics shared than John F. Kennedy. What Catholic will ever forget his address to the Greater Houston Ministerial Association, on September 12, 1960, in which he declared:[18]

> I believe in an America where the separation of Church and state is absolute — where no Catholic prelate would tell the President, should he be a Catholic, how to act .... I believe in a President whose views on religion are his own private affair ...

It was only by J.F.K.'s great personal gifts and by the inherent fair-mindedness of the American people that he was able to win the 1960 American presidential election, albeit narrowly. But if no one suffered more, no one contributed more to the ultimate resolution of the problem. The whole world watched the drama of 1960 unfold, and Catholics around the world became determined to ensure that Catholic politicians should never again be placed in the invidious position of having their political integrity questioned because of their Catholic faith.

Five years later at the end of Vatican II — too late, sadly, for President Kennedy to enjoy his triumph — the doctrine of religious freedom as a fundamental human right was proclaimed in the *Declaration on Religious Freedom* (*Dignitatis Humanae Personae*). John Courtney Murray, who is generally given credit for having written the document, commented wryly :[19]

> It can hardly be maintained that the *Declaration* is a milestone in human history — moral, political or intellectual. The principle of religious freedom has long been recognized in constitutional law, to the point where even Marxist-Leninist political ideology is obliged to pay lip-service to it. In all honesty it must be admitted that the Church is late in acknowledging the validity of the principle.

⚬⚬

The doctrinal substance of the *Declaration on Religious Freedom* is set out at the very beginning of its first chapter, the first constituent paragraph stating the content of the right to religious freedom, i.e., freedom from human coercion, the second the source of this right:[20]

General Principle of Religious Freedom

2. This Vatican Synod declares that the human person has a right to religious freedom. This freedom means that all men are to be immune from coercion on the part of individuals or of social groups and of any human power, in such wise that in matters religious no one is to be forced to act in a manner contrary to his own beliefs. Nor is anyone to be restrained from acting in accordance with his own beliefs, whether privately or publicly, whether alone or in association with others, within due limits.

The Synod further declares that the right to religious freedom has its foundation in the very dignity of the human person, as this dignity is known through the revealed Word of God and by reason itself. This right of the human person to religious freedom is to be recognized in the constitutional law whereby society is governed. Thus it is to become a civil right.

People are, of course, obliged in conscience to seek the objective truth, but the existence of their political right to freedom of religion exists independently of how they are exercising their liberty:[21]

It is in accordance with their dignity as persons — that is, beings endowed with reason and free will and therefore privileged to bear personal responsibility — that all men should be at once impelled by nature and also bound by a moral obligation to seek the truth, especially religious truth. They are also bound to adhere to the truth, once it is known, and to order their whole lives in accord with the demands of truth.

However, men cannot discharge these obligations in a manner in keeping with their own nature unless they enjoy immunity from external coercion as well as psychological freedom. Therefore, the right to religious freedom has its foundation, not in the subjective disposition of the person, but in his very nature. In consequence, the right to this immunity continues to exist even in those who do not live up to their obligation of seeking the truth and adhering to it. Nor is the exercise of this right to be impeded, provided that the just requirements of public order are observed.

The right to religious freedom, although said to be one that should be recognized constitutionally by every state, is rested in the *Declaration* primarily on the ethical foundation of the right itself.

Government has the obligation not only of safeguarding the right of religious freedom but also of creating favourable conditions for its exercise:[22]

The protection and promotion of the inviolable rights of man ranks among the essential duties of government. Therefore, government is to assume the safeguard of the religious freedom of all its citizens, in an effective manner, by just laws and by other appropriate means. Government is also to help create conditions favourable to the fostering of religious life, in order that the people may be truly enabled to exercise their religious rights and to fulfil their religious duties, and also in order that society itself may profit by the moral qualities of justice and peace which have their origin in men's faithfulness to God and to His holy will.

The government's duty to protect and promote human rights is part of its care of the common good. It is not defined in detail, since that is the province of the state rather than of the church. All that is specified is the principle of a free society:[23]

[T]he usages of society are to be the usages of freedom in their full range. These require that the freedom of man be respected as far as possible, and curtailed only when and in so far as necessary.

The "establishment" of a state religion, as it exists by historical circumstance in the United Kingdom, continues to be permitted, provided that such establishment does not trench on the religious liberties of citizens of other faiths:[24]

> If, in view of peculiar circumstances obtaining among certain peoples, special legal recognition is given in the constitutional order of society to one religious body, it is at the same time imperative that the right of all citizens and religious bodies to religious freedom should be recognized and made effective in practice.

The freedom which is recognized in the *Declaration* is specifically that of religion rather than that of conscience. Needless to say, although the two differ in concept, with religion adding to conscience the extra "note" or element of the external practice of cult, or acts of prayer or devotion, there is also a lot of overlap, and the two should not be sharply distinguished. Certainly, since freedom of religion is the more encompassing, everything said by way of recognition of that right must be logically true also of the right of conscience at the political level, though it should be understood that the *Declaration* does not base the right to free exercise of religion on freedom of conscience, no doubt because of the dangers in moral thought of a subjective notion of conscience.

Nevertheless, one distinction made in the *Declaration* is of capital importance. As will be seen in a careful reading of the very first paragraph of the *Declaration* quoted *supra*, conscience or religious freedom is absolute when it is a question of not being forced to act in a way contrary to it: "in matters religious no one is to be forced to act in a manner contrary to his own beliefs." For want of a better term, I shall call this "conscience negatively expressed" or "negative conscience." It corresponds to the "freedom from" view taken by most fundamental statements of human rights. On the other hand, "freedom for," the right to act freely in accordance with one's beliefs, is a slightly qualified right: "Nor is anyone to be restrained from acting in accordance with his own beliefs ... *within due limits.*" I call this "conscience positively expressed" or "positive conscience."(emphasis mine)

The Council fathers made no attempt to spell out all of the implications and consequences of the *Declaration*, such as the meaning of "due limits." Much was left to the good sense of politicians. All was left open to the progress of thought and civilization. As John Courtney Murray put it:[25]

> The conciliar affirmation of the principle of freedom was narrowly limited — in the text. But the text itself was flung into a pool whose shores are wide as the universal church. The ripples will run far.

In his commentary on the *Declaration*, John Courtney Murray also informs us that it was "the most controversial document of the whole Council."[26] The reason it was such was the necessity of overruling by implication the *Syllabus of Errors*. It was, he says, "the notion of development [of doctrine], not the notion of religion freedom, [that] was the real sticking-point for many of those who opposed the *Declaration* even to the end."[27] The victory represented by the *Declaration* in the field of church-state relations has therefore even larger significance for the future of Catholic theology, including the future of *Humanae Vitae*.

Behind this question of the development of doctrine lies the theory of John Henry Newman that a dogmatic idea must not be confused with its many expressions or aspects. Not only is "no one aspect deep enough to exhaust the contents of a real idea, no one term or proposition which will serve to define it,"[28] but there is a process of development "by which the aspects of an idea are brought into consistency and form ... being the germination and maturation of some truth or apparent truth on a large mental field."[29] An idea "is dependent in various ways on the circumstances which surround it."[30] Relevant kinds of development which may occur are political, logical, historical, ethical and metaphysical. Although not open-ended, dogma is progressively revealed, and earlier attempts to state it may have to be superseded by more mature wisdom. There may even have been a false start, as in the case of the *Syllabus of Errors*.

CHAPTER 7

CONSCIENCE, THE FIRST OF DEMOCRATIC RIGHTS

The first country in history to *begin* the long journey towards constitutionalism and democracy was not the United States but the United Kingdom — or England, as it then was, if we go back as far as Magna Carta in 1215 for our starting point. English history was characterized by a seemingly interminable struggle among king, nobles and commons, in which the monarchs gradually got the upper hand over the barons and were then ultimately tamed by the representatives of the people.

England supposedly became a constitutional monarchy with the "Glorious" Revolution in 1688 but the king's hand was still very directly and heavily involved in government throughout the reign of George III. Nevertheless, the forms of constitutionalism and parliamentarianism existed throughout the eighteenth century, to the point that Montesquieu wrote an analysis of British practice of the day which became the foundation of American government, and so of the first realized democracy in a major society. Unfortunately for historical accuracy, Montesquieu's division of powers failed to take account of the unity between the executive branch and the majority in the legislative branch, and his separation of the three powers, although it may be said to have served Americans well, was based on a rather significant misunderstanding of the British (no longer "English" after 1701) system. Hence the United Kingdom and most of the rest of the English-speaking world have remained with a system of responsible government (i.e., cabinet responsible to legislature), whereas the United States began its new experiment with a presidential system and a separation of powers.

Whether endowed with a presidential or a prime ministerial system, in the twentieth century most democracies have chosen to emulate the United States in having not only a written constitution but also a written fundamental law which guarantees the liberties of the people from both executive and legislative infringement. In Britain the opposition now talks about the desirability of constitutionalized rights, and even now Britain is subject to the European Convention on Human Rights.[1] In Canada, a Charter of Rights and Liberties came into effect on 17 April 1982, close to two hundred years after the U S Bill of Rights, which is the collective name for the first ten amendments to the U.S. Constitution. Such people's charters provide protection not only against executive action, but also against legislative infringement of rights.

⚜

Constitutional bills of rights are generally similar in having a list of the protected rights or freedoms, and often there are justificatory provisions as to when a *prima facie* breach is nevertheless justifiable. The United States has no explicit provision for justification of such apparent infringements, whereas the very first section of the Canadian Charter provides that:

> 1. The *Canadian Charter of Rights and Freedoms* guarantees the rights and freedoms set out in it subject only to such reasonable limits prescribed by law as can be demonstrably justified in a free and democratic society.

Not only does this provision provide a means by which government can prove that infringing legislation or action is not ultimately in violation of the Charter, but it also effectively denominates Canada as "a free and democratic society."

Fundamental freedoms in Canada are protected by section 2 of the Charter, which reads as follows:

> 2. Everyone has the following fundamental freedoms:
> (a) freedom of conscience and religion;
> (b) freedom of thought, belief, opinion and expression, including freedom of the press and other media of communication;
> (c) freedom of peaceful assembly; and
> (d) freedom of association.

The great American judge, Justice Benjamin Cardozo, thought that "freedom of thought, and speech ... is the matrix, the indispensable condition of nearly every other form of freedom."[2] In my view, he was correct in thinking that freedom of thought and speech is the most comprehensive freedom, and in that sense the most fundamental. However, as I see it, the freedom of conscience is truly the most fundamental of the freedoms, as the most personal, the most interior, and the most precious.

The U.S. Bill of Rights has the distinction of being the oldest still-current expression of fundamental rights, but is now "behind the times" in not explicitly recognizing the right of conscience.[3] In the aftermath of the Second World War, the freedom of conscience was very much on people's minds, and it was characterized as a fundamental freedom in 1948 by Article 18 of the Universal Declaration of Human Rights, which reads as follows:

> 18. Everyone has the right to freedom of thought, conscience and religion; this right includes freedom to change his religion or belief, and freedom, alone or in community with others and in public or private, to manifest his religion or belief in teaching, practice, worship and observance.

The other fundamental freedoms follow in Articles 19 and 20.

The successor international document, the International Covenant on Civil and Political Rights, came into effect in 1976 and was later ratified by both Canada and the United States. Article 18 again provides that "everyone shall have the right to freedom of thought, conscience and religion."

The most significant regional document, the European Convention on Human Rights, which came into effect in 1950, was based on the Universal Declaration and on a very early draft of the Covenant. It provides in Article 9 that "everyone has the right to freedom of thought, conscience and religion," and, again, the statement of this right precedes that of the freedom of expression (Article 10) and the freedom of peaceful assembly and freedom of association (Article 10).

It is evident from these three documents that conscience is not intended to be oriented only towards religion, since it is also linked with freedom of thought, which is certainly not limited to a religious ambit. The Canadian Charter of Rights and Freedoms lists the freedom of thought separately from that of conscience and religion, perhaps on the theory that "thought" is the germ of expression, as conscience is of religion. In any event, the only stated link of the freedom of conscience is to religion, but I am of the view that it should not be seen in the context only of religion. Although Chief Justice Dickson in *R. v. Big M. Drug Mart* referred to "the single integrated concept of freedom of conscience and religion,"[4] he also made it clear that he did not intend that the meaning of conscience should be governed by the concept of religion, and that the irreligious as well as the religious have the benefit of freedom of conscience.[5]

This was emphatically the view of Justice Bertha Wilson in the Supreme Court. Commenting on the Chief Justice's phrase, she stated:[6]

The Chief Justice sees religious belief and practice as the paradigmatic example of conscientiously-held beliefs and manifestations and as such protected by the Charter. But I do not think he is saying that a personal morality which is not founded in religion is outside the protection of s. 2(a) [of the Charter] ...

It seems to me ... that in a free and democratic society "freedom of conscience and religion" should be broadly construed to extend to conscientiously-held beliefs, whether grounded in religion or in a secular morality. Indeed, as a matter of statutory interpretation, "conscience" and "religion" should not be treated as tautologous, if capable of independent, although related, meanings.

I am in complete agreement. However, for purposes of my philosophical argument it is not necessary that the freedom of conscience have a legally recognized position in any particular constitution.

The place of conscience was recently recognized by Pope John Paul II when he wrote that "the recognition of these rights [the rights of the human conscience] represents the primary foundation of every authentically free political order."[7] That was apparently also the view of Chief Justice Dickson in the first important Charter case in Canada, the *Big M. Drug Mart* case, where he reflected on the democratic political tradition:[8]

What unites enunciated freedoms in the American First Amendment, s. 2(*a*) of the *Charter* and in the provisions of other human rights documents in which they are associated is *the notion of the centrality of individual conscience and the inappropriateness of governmental intervention to compel or to constrain its manifestation.* In *Hunter* v. *Southam Inc.* [[1984] 2 S.C.R. 145], the purpose of the *Charter* was identified, at p. 155, as "the unremitting protection of individual rights and liberties". It is easy to see the relationship between respect for individual conscience and the valuation of human dignity that motivates such unremitting protection.

It should also be noted, however, that *an emphasis on individual conscience and individual judgment also lies at the heart of our democratic political tradition.* The ability of each citizen to make free and informed decisions is the absolute prerequisite for the legitimacy, acceptability, and efficacy of our system of self-government. It is because of *the centrality of the rights associated with freedom of individual conscience both to basic beliefs about human worth and dignity and to a free and democratic political system* that American jurisprudence has emphasized the primacy or "firstness" of the first Amendment. It is this same centrality that in my view underlies their designation in the *Canadian Charter of Rights and Freedoms* as "fundamental". They are the *sine qua non* of the political tradition underlying the Charter.

Viewed in this context, the purpose of freedom of conscience and religion becomes clear. The values that underlie our political and philosophic traditions demand that every individual be free to hold and to manifest whatever beliefs and opinions his or her conscience dictates, provided *inter alia* only that such manifestations do not injure his or her neighbours or their parallel rights to hold and manifest beliefs, and opinions of their own. Religious beliefs and practice are historically prototypical, and, in many ways, paradigmatic of conscientiously-held beliefs and manifestations and are therefore protected by the Charter. Equally protected, and for the same reasons are expressions and manifestations of religious non-belief and refusals to participate in religious practice. (emphasis added)

I am particularly struck by Chief Justice Dickson's several references to the centrality of individual conscience and to "the centrality of the rights associated with freedom of individual conscience both to basic beliefs about human worth and dignity and to a free and democratic political system." The right of conscience is to my mind the heart of human dignity because it touches human beings in their most vulnerable and inward relationships, those in relation to a Supreme Being on whom they recognize their dependence, or to a principle of ethical behaviour which is the lodestar of their existence.[9] Only pure thought is similarly interior, and I would assimilate it to conscience if it contains an organizing principle of ethical life, i.e., if it is action-directed in a principled way amounting to an ethic. Expression, assembly and association concern themselves with outward manifestations of the inner person. Even religion, if distinguished from conscience, is an external expression of the inmost self.

But conscience is that very self, the wellspring of all other life and thought. In this I am very much of the same mind as Lord Acton, viz., that conscience is the only political absolute, and that the other liberties, important as they are to the human spirit, are accurately enough thought of as the "domain" of conscience, expressing in various kinds of activity what flows from conscience, the inner light.

Whatever the merits of a right of "privacy," they do not in my usage strike this deeply, although it seems that by privacy its American proponents increasingly have in mind very much what in my conception is more accurately embraced in conscience. Even in one of the earlier Supreme Court decisions Justice Cardozo stated that the Due Process Clause protects those liberties that are "so rooted in the traditions *and conscience* of our people as to be ranked as fundamental."[10] (emphasis added) Very recently, in their joint opinion in *Casey*, Justices O'Connor, Kennedy and Souter wrote:[11]

> These matters, involving the most intimate and personal choices a person may make in a lifetime, choices central to personal dignity and autonomy, are central to the liberty protected by the Fourteenth Amendment. At the heart of liberty is the right to define one's own concept of existence, of meaning, of the universe, and of the mystery of human life. Beliefs about these matters could not define the attributes of personhood were they formed under compulsion of the State.

This is language that could very well be used of freedom of conscience. If that is what privacy means, then it may well be indistinguishable from freedom of conscience as I understand it.

In its philosophical sense conscience is essentially synonymous with the virtue of prudence, as the act which completes that virtue or habit. The abstract name "prudence" is today often used as a synonym for "caution," and in French that seems to be its ordinary meaning, whereas its root word is the Latin *providentia*, providence. In the Shorter Oxford English Dictionary (1984), prudence is defined as the "ability to discern the most suitable, politic, or profitable cause of action, especially as regards conduct; practical wisdom; discretion."

For some philosophers prudence is the pre-eminent moral virtue. Josef Pieper, for whose views I have much respect, writes that :[12]

> Prudence is the *cause* of the other virtues being virtues at all. For example, there may be a kind of instinctive governance of instinctual cravings; but only prudence transforms

> this instinctive governance into the "virtue" of temperance ...
>
> Prudence is the "*measure*" of justice, of fortitude, of temperance ... What is prudent and what is good are substantially one and the same; they differ only in their place in the logical succession of realization. For whatever is good must first have been prudent.
>
> Prudence "informs" [in the Aristotelian sense of "constitutes"] the other virtues; it confers upon them the form of their inner essence.

The moral status of prudence is such that Pieper maintains that "nothing less than the whole ordered structure of the Occidental Christian view of man rests upon the pre-eminence of prudence over the other virtues."[13] Prudence is particularly closely related to justice, because that is where it is principally manifested.

The standard of prudence, in turn, is the objective reality of being. In scholastic terminology, being (i.e., reality) precedes truth (which is the realm of prudence or conscience), which precedes goodness. Prudence therefore looks two ways, towards both intellect and will — it looks to being for cognition and towards action in decision. In other words, it is both cognitive and volitional. It is the knowing aspect which most directly reveals its status as "conscience" (a word ultimately linked with the Latin *scientia*, knowledge). By prudence or conscience the knowledge of what is the best to do (i.e., truest to reality) is directed to concrete realization.

The correctness of prudence or conscience in the case of any person will depend on the correctness of that person's perception of reality and his/her corresponding rectitude in turning that perception into action. People thus have a moral obligation to make themselves as knowledgeable as possible about correct behaviour and to act as effectively as possible on the basis of that knowledge.

But by their very nature prudential decisions are directed to actions to be performed here and now, by the person confronted with the decision. Pope John Paul II has written:

> Conscience is ... an act of a person's intelligence, the function of which is to apply the universal knowledge of the good in a specific situation and thus to express a judgment about the right conduct to beckon here and now, to be chosen.[14]

A person's conscience, and that alone, determines the subjective "rightness" of an act. No one else can gainsay, from the subjective point of view, the morality of a person's actions. Pieper writes that "there is no way of grasping the concreteness of a man's ethical decisions from outside."[15] The only *entrée* at all into a person's moral life is through the love of friendship, because through love a kind of internal visualization (empathy) of the concrete situation of the other person is possible. The first principle of the moral life may therefore be said to be "my conscience, right or wrong!"

Conscience is thus the heart of morality. It is also, if I am right in my analysis, the foremost of the human rights that the state is pledged to protect through the guarantees of fundamental freedoms now generally recognized to be as intrinsic to democracy as is majority rule. Democracy, by its own inner dynamic, recognizes the freedom of conscience as its most sacred trust, arriving in its own way at the same first principle discovered by morality as its ultimate criterion.

⚘

In a democracy, as I have indicated, there are actually two fundamental principles, individual freedoms (crystallized, above all, in conscience) and majority rights, and so a balance must be struck in a societal context, according to the lines already suggested by the *Declaration on Religious Freedom* through the distinction within conscience between "freedom from" and "freedom for." Conscience's status as the first principle of democracy is manifested primarily through negative conscience, where it holds absolute sway over the majoritarian principle.

It is, I think, now a matter of general acceptance in democratic societies, that there is an absolute exemption of conscience from being forced to do anything of a personal nature contrary to it, whether in the form of compulsion to believe, to appreciate, to worship or whatever else might constrain the conscience.[16] It is in this spirit that I interpret the U.S. Supreme Court decision in *West Virginia Board of Education* v. *Barnette*[17] to invalidate a compulsory flag salute statute challenged by Jehovah's Witnesses.

There would also, I believe, be general agreement that such freedom from constraint does not extend to a person's property. A person who conscientiously believes that his income is beyond the reach of the state may nevertheless be compelled to pay taxes in the public interest, for the privilege of living in the society. Indeed, this is not at all a matter of negative conscience, since property can be alienated by law with no implication of personal commitment.

However, there are no absolute zones of freedom when the question is one of "freedom for," of positive conscience, as I have called it. The *Declaration on Religious Freedom*, considered in chapter 6, expressed it this way: "Nor is anyone to be restrained from acting in accordance with his own beliefs, whether privately or publicly, whether alone or in association with others, *within due limits*."[18] (emphasis added) The *Declaration* gave no guidance to the state as to how these due limits are to be established. As it was put recently by John Paul II, "the Church respects *the legitimate autonomy of the democratic order*, and is not entitled to express preferences for this or that institutional or constitutional solution."[19]

In the United States the Supreme Court has been closely divided in recent cases on the scope of the free exercise of religion clause in the First Amendment. In *Employment Division* v. *Smith*,[20] which involved the sacramental use of peyote in the Native American Church, a bare majority of the Court (per Scalia J.) held that the free exercise clause did not relieve from the obligation to comply with neutral laws of general applicability which impinged on religious practice. Since there was no suggestion of the necessity of a compelling state interest to justify interference, barring an open governmental attack on religion, Professor Stephen L. Carter has described this as a "horrible ... decision" which might allow the free exercise clause to disappear.[21] Three years later, in *Church of Lukumi Babalu Aye, Inc.* v. *City of Hialiah*,[22] the Court struck down city ordinances prohibiting the ritual slaughter of animals, ordinances which it found to have as their direct object the suppression of the Santeria religion. Almost at the same time, in *Lamb's Chapel* v. *Center Moriches Union Free School District*,[23] the Court decided another case which appeared inconsistent with *Smith*, but again without re-examining that case. Personally, I agree with Professor Carter that the desirable free exercise rule would be to require "the state to carry a heavy burden, perhaps even a compelling one, as its regulation strikes closer and closer to the heart of the religious tradition in question,"[24] so that religions unable to protect themselves in the political process are not doomed to destruction.

American experience would thus suggest that the "due limits" to positive conscience are not easily subject to principled determination, but I would recall that the other principle against which they are to be balanced is that of majority rule. The balancing has therefore to be found, in part, in the number of those who hold a particular conscientious position. In that way a reconciliation of both principles can be partially achieved. However, in my view, in cases of doubt, priority must be given to conscience, as the more personal and human principle, over the principle of the social mass.

With respect to positive conscience, what I have in mind is this. The modern state, with its large numbers of people, cannot possibly give room for positive expression in every matter to the demands of every individual conscience. For every kind of recognition of its positive manifestations there must be a determinate number of people with a sufficiently significant demand to warrant the public expenditure required (if any is), the inconvenience to others, or even the legislative or administrative accommodation it may make necessary. A city, for instance, does not need to divert traffic because one or two people wish to conduct a ceremony in the middle of the street, but where hundreds want peaceably to assemble, to demonstrate, to hold a parade or have a procession, the result must be different.

In direct proportion to the degree of inconvenience involved to other people, or to government administration itself, the number of people who want *positively* to express their right of conscience in a particular way must, to be justifiable, be of sufficient size. I think it is not, however, possible exactly to quantify the requirements of minimum participation.

Whether abortion is an expression of negative or positive conscience is a serious question with enormous consequences. If looked at from the point of view of the aborted fetus, it is an aggressive act of the strongest sort, causing its destruction. Considered from the side of the pregnant woman, it is simply not requiring her to carry her pregnancy to full term, in circumstances where in her opinion that would be inappropriate.

However, the fact that arguments can be made on both sides does not mean that the choice between them can be made arbitrarily by the toss of a coin or even that it is morally marginal. As I see it, the answer is based on the natural order itself.

In this sense, what we have first to take into account is the fact that until viability the mother and the fetus have to share the mother's body (using it in different ways). Most important is the fact that the only conscience is that of the mother. Since the freedom of this conscience is in question, the only viewpoint until viability can be that of this conscience, so that the issue is whether this conscience can be forced to act in a way contrary to its beliefs, viz., to continue a pregnancy which for perceived good reasons of conscience has become unwanted. From this point of view abortion is a matter of negative freedom, which is an absolute freedom, and not subject to intrinsic legislative limitation.

However, after viability, when the fetus with its conscience can survive on its own apart from the mother's body, the question becomes one of positive conscience, and the justification for abortion would have to be on a different and more limited basis. Where, as in most Western societies today, a majority of the people or a very large minority believe that the law must permit abortion even after viability for therapeutic purposes (i.e., to save the mother's life or health) in order that their rights of conscience be fulfilled, I am led to conclude that society must accept that claim but only insofar as an abortion is therapeutic. By this I have in mind that priority must be given to the positive freedom of conscience where the proposed positive exercise is genuine and where it is so generally demanded that it can claim the support of a large part of the population, but only insofar as the precise welfare of the mother (i.e., life or health) is concerned. After viability, abortion must be a qualified rather than an absolute right, limited to therapeutic situations.

Why should viability rather than birth itself make a difference in the basis on which abortion is available, and, if it should be so taken into account, why should it not then have the effect of precluding abortion altogether? In my excursus on the moral considerations in abortion in chapter 2, it was not viability but the period shortly after conception which I found to be the starting point of human life. Moreover, viability is more a statistical concept than a precise point in human gestation: although a fetus is assumed to be viable about the twenty-fourth week of pregnancy, the survival rate at that point is low, and rises only slowly during the rest of the normal term of forty weeks.

Nevertheless, whenever viability may occur as a matter of fact, in theory there is a difference in kind between a fetus before and after viability. At birth, of course, the unique relationship between mother and child comes to an end, with the child then relying on his/her own circulatory and digestive system for continuance in existence, but viability is a kind of anticipated birth in that it is the point at which the child can first survive outside the mother's body.

It is crucial to distinguish two possible justifications for induced abortion: (1) freeing the mother from the burden of carrying the fetus to term, and (2) destroying the fetus. There is a close but not a necessary connection between the two. A women's right to abortion is a right to be unburdened of the fetus, not the right to destroy it as such, even though the carrying out of the first before viability will always lead to the second. The purpose for which abortion is allowable by the state, however, is not that of depriving the fetus of life, but only of ending its life-support system in the mother's body. Professor Harry W. Wellington has rightly written:[25]

> If the woman's right to an abortion included the right to demand the death of the fetus, viability would be irrelevant ... But the woman has no such right: the death of a fetus from abortion is a consequence of the woman's having exercised a right based on and coextensive with the principle that she may decide what happens in or to her body.

Even after viability, the difference is more theoretical than practical, because the usual methods of abortion in current medical practice, viz., dilatation and curettage (D&C), vacuum aspiration, and dilatation and evacuation (D&E, the most likely technique for a late abortion), all invariably kill the fetus at any stage of its existence. (Only the rarely used technique of abdominal incision — hysterotomy — does not involve advance destruction of the fetus.) Even if the methods used did not immediately destroy the fetus, before viability the fetus could not in any event survive outside the uterus.

Nevertheless, I repeat that the mother's right to abortion does not include the right to destroy the fetus as such. It is only that the inevitable effect of abortion is fetal destruction, given the fetus' inability to survive. Once the factor of viability comes into play, however, the situation is different. No longer are there two beings which can survive only through one body. There are henceforth two beings with two incipiently separated bodies, and the wanton destruction of a separated — or in the process of being separated — fetus (about to be a prematurely born infant) would be akin to infanticide.

The saving of a fetus after viability is more a theoretical possibility than a practical likelihood, both because abortions are rarely performed beyond the point of fetal viability,[26] and because the usual methods of abortion yield in any event a dead fetus. But it is important to emphasize, in a philosophical reflection on the law, that different considerations must apply after viability.

Professor L.W. Sumner, who establishes the presence of feeling or sensation as his criterion of moral standing, agrees that "viability can ... serve as a (rough) indicator of moral standing."[27] He therefore has to take a position on the distinct grounds for abortion after viability:[28]

> Legal grounds for late abortion are a special case of conditions for justifiable homicide. As much as possible (allowing for the unique relation between mother and fetus) these grounds should authorize abortion when killing would also be justified in relevantly similar cases not involving fetuses.

He dismisses the categories of humanitarian grounds (pregnancy due to the commission of a crime such as rape or incest) and socio-economic grounds (poverty, family size, etc.), but recognizes those of therapeutic grounds (threat to maternal life or health) and eugenic grounds (fetal abnormality). Though my own process of reasoning is somewhat different, I accept his conclusion as to the retention of therapeutic grounds for abortion:[29]

> Therapeutic grounds for abortion follow from a woman's right of self-defence. The threat, however, must be serious in two different respects: the injury in prospect must be more

than trivial and the probability of its occurrence must be greater than normal. The risks generally associated with pregnancy will not here suffice. Further, there must be good medical reason not to delay until the fetus has a better chance of survival, and every effort must be made to save the fetus' life if this is possible. Thus late abortion for therapeutic reasons ought to be reserved for genuine medical emergencies in which no other action would qualify as proper care of the mother. In many putatively moderate policies therapeutic grounds for abortion (especially mental health clauses) are interpreted so liberally as to cover large numbers of cases that are not by any stretch of the imagination medical emergencies.

Although Professor Sumner has a similarly strict interpretation of eugenic grounds, I cannot agree with him on their inclusion, which he puts on the same basis as euthanasia for defective newborns, a concept which I also do not accept, for reasons which will become more apparent in my consideration of euthanasia in chapter 10.

In fine, I agree with Professor Sumner that from the state's point of view "an early abortion is ... a private transaction between a woman and her physician,"[30] like a decision on contraception. At this stage, the woman's autonomy is absolute, and legislation may merely regulate the quality of medical care, not establish grounds for her access to abortion.

With respect to post-viability abortions, however, the state must establish grounds in terms of the life and health of the mother, and in my view these grounds should be narrowly drawn. The state may not, of course, simply require that the fetus be delivered alive, as a premature infant, since of the currently available methods of abortion only hysterotomy could possibly produce that result, and it involves major surgery akin to a caesarian operation which could threaten the mother's life or health. Nevertheless, in my opinion legislation should ensure that if the fetus emerges alive (a more likely eventuality in the United States than in Canada because of the later abortions there), every effort be made to resuscitate and maintain its life as in any case of premature delivery.[31] On the one hand, such a baby would have to be considered a ward of the state rather than a child the mother could be required to accept; on the other hand the parents would have to be frustrated in their desire to destroy their "genetic material," if such were their desire. To give free rein to such a desire would, in fact, be tantamount to encouraging infanticide. As Professor Judith Jarvis Thomson has written, "the desire for the child's death is not one which anybody may gratify, should it turn out to be possible to detach the child alive."[32]

The other issue of conscience which will immediately come to mind is that of Jehovah's Witnesses and blood transfusions. I should say that I very much agree with the decision of Mr. Justice Robins for the Ontario Court of Appeal that an adult Jehovah's Witness is entitled to reject blood transfusions because "people must have the right to make choices that accord with their own values regardless of how unwise or foolish those choices may appear to others."[33] This is, in fact, a recognition of the conscience principle, as the court recognized: "to transfuse a Jehovah's Witness in the face of her explicit instructions to the contrary would, in my opinion, violate her right to control her own body and show disrespect for the religious values by which she has chosen to live her life."[34]

The result must be entirely different where the life in question is that of a child of a Jehovah's Witness. There, the normal rule requiring parental consent for surgical procedures to their children is superseded by the legal doctrine of necessity.[35] Moreover, custody of the child will be removed from any parent who wilfully withholds needed medical care.[36]

In sum, once a fetus can have an independent life (and obviously much more so after birth in the Jehovah's Witnesses cases), the mere convenience of the mother cannot alone determine the result. Where the mother's conscience is set-off against a life-and-death effect on an emerged or emergent human being (due to birth or the capability of birth), it can be exercised only within due limits. Where the danger to the mother is to her own life or health, her freedom of conscience must have priority, but not where lesser claims on her behalf are in question.

The priority of the mother's conscience (even after viability where her life or health is in question) is in my opinion not only sound theory but also a matter of elementary common sense. It must be obvious that where a very large number of citizens is involved, the imposition and implementation of coercive legislation, which could cost the mother her life or health as well as infringe upon her conscience, simply would not be feasible, not even to save fetal life. Democracy cannot run on mass coercion, and law must be at least tolerable to the consciences of the vast majority of its citizens. This is particularly true when the law that is in question is essentially coercive criminal law. However, this consideration of practicability is secondary to the governing principle of conscience.

Until viability, the mother's conscience cannot be constrained so as to compel her to complete her pregnancy. Where her conscience so directs, she must be free to terminate her pregnancy. The situation, from the viewpoint of conscience, changes only at viability. Then the normal constraints on positive conscience in society come into play.

CHAPTER 8

CRIMINAL LAW AND ABORTION

A s discussed in chapter 4, there seems to be very general agreement in our society that the proper domain of the criminal law is behaviour that causes harm to other people, i.e., anti-social conduct rather than behaviour which is harmful only to oneself. So individual vices like alcoholism and addiction are considered inappropriate matters for criminal legislation except insofar as they have social repercussions. Obscenity falls under criminal proscription in that it is deemed to induce sexually aggressive conduct towards others (though it must be admitted that, in social science terms, this is not yet conclusively established).

In these terms, pro-life proponents argue, abortion is an extreme form of anti-social conduct, since it involves the destruction of other human beings, and no Christian legislator could conceivably allow it. In this vein Professor William E. Carroll has asked:[1]

> How would we respond to a politician who says that he is personally opposed to rape but does not wish to pass a law prohibiting it, because such a law would interfere with the right of the rapist to commit rape? If the opposition to rape is because of what rape is — the doing of sexual violence to another human being — then automatically the matter has to be public and not private. Or what of a politician who maintains that he is personally opposed to stealing but is unwilling to pass laws prohibiting theft because in so doing he would be imposing his own moral judgements on others? The poverty of such arguments is apparent. They not only confuse private and public morality, but are also logically inconsistent.

But in fact, depending on who categorizes it, abortion may be regarded as either social or individual behaviour. If the fetus is considered a human person with full human rights at the time of abortion, then its destruction is obviously an anti-social act, and abortion is appropriate for prohibitory criminal legislation. But if, as the majority in our society see it, the aborted fetus is either not a human being, or at least not a human person with full civil rights until birth, then the act of abortion is a matter of private morality in which only the interests of the mother should be taken into account, and criminal prohibition is wrong.

Professor Carroll's real argument is not with the Catholic politician whose view of the common good is different from his own. It is rather with the consciences of the majority who "stubbornly" resist his moral perspective.

Recent history makes it clear, I believe, that there is no way in which a social consensus can be reached on the substance of this profound disagreement. No middle point between the extremes can be found because the law must be one way or the other. The question is whether we are going to allow it to poison the whole of our political life. The only hope for resolution, as I see it, is that we find sufficient agreement at the level of process, i.e., in relation to our respect for one another's consciences.

Why should it be Catholics who give way when a social impasse has been reached? If that is the consequence of my theory, it is only because Catholic preferences are the overly inclusive views as to the law in this case. To understand this, let us distinguish among concentric circles of conscience.

In its strictest sense conscience refers only to one person's here-and-now practical judgment about that person's immediate action. At a first level of generalization, it gives scope also to that person's future actions of the same kind. Then, at another level of generalization it refers to actions of the same kind by other people of the same mind. At this level of generalization (as well as at the two previous ones) we can still speak of freedom of conscience, a range of moral decision making untrammelled by governmental constraint.

However, there is a further level of generalization at which conscience attempts to become its brother's keeper, where it concerns itself with actions by non-like-minded people who are engaging in actions which the conscience considers to be morally wrong on an objective basis. Of course, this is not seen — or at least not presented — as an attempt to interfere with others' consciences, but only as an effort to guarantee an objective good — in the case of abortion, the lives of unborn human beings.

But in fact those lives, although real enough, are still incubated in the bodies of women with consciences of their own. There is no way of getting to the unborn except through the bodies and consciences of those women. There is no way for an outside conscience to protect the unborn, therefore, except through the consciences of those women — or through constraint applied by the state to them. Such constraint is precisely what must be avoided if we are to have freedom of conscience.

In other words, it is at this point that the freedom of one conscience and that of another would conflict if one were given such extension as allowed it to control the other on the basis of protecting the unborn child. Such an understanding of the freedom of the controlling conscience cannot be defended as a legitimate expression of freedom of conscience but must be recognized for what it would be, viz., the imposition of the practical judgments of that conscience on those of another. It would no longer be freedom of conscience, but rather tyranny of conscience.

Christians cannot have it both ways. While the Church has never "canonized" democracy as the perfect form of government, and must always retain what Professor R.A. Markus has called "the duty to refuse absoluteness to every finite and relative claim in this world,"[2] nevertheless democracy is without question the form of government most compatible with Christianity. John Paul II has recently indicated how much the Church values democracy:[3]

> 46. The Church values the democratic system inasmuch as it ensures the participation of citizens in making political choices, guarantees to the governed the possibility both of electing and holding accountable those who govern them, and of replacing them through peaceful means when appropriate.

In this statement he is in continuity with the views expressed some years earlier by Pope John XXIII, that "the dignity of the human person involves ... the right to take an active part in public affairs and to contribute one's part to the common good of the citizens."[4] Both statements echo the views of St. Thomas Aquinas in the thirteenth century that all should have a share in the government (chapter 5).[5]

If Christians want democracy for their own purposes, they must take it according to its own internal dynamic. They cannot enjoy democracy only while it produces the results they want, and adopt a different system that produces more congenial results the rest of the time.

Governor Mario Cuomo was, in my opinion, stating the democratic dynamic as it is when he declared that American Catholics "realize that in guaranteeing freedom for all, they guarantee *our* right to be Catholics, our *right* to pray, to use the sacraments ... to reject abortion ..." And again: "to assure our freedom we must allow others the same freedom."[6]

If we look at the problem of abortion from the viewpoint of the legislator rather than of the citizen, I believe the result is the same. In view of the common good, Catholic legislators cannot look only to what they believe in their consciences to be right, but must also consider what others believe in conscience with equal firmness to be right. Sometimes a temporary accommodation can be reached, as we in Canada enjoyed for two decades on abortion, but even this was achieved only at the price of Catholic legislators' acknowledging their lack of authority — moral and legal — to constrain others' consciences.

If no accommodation is possible and the legislators are immediately at the great divide, or if the existing accommodation breaks down, as it ultimately did in Canada, then the largest issue must be faced. On the one hand, the prohibition of abortion would directly infringe on the consciences of those who believe they are morally impelled to have abortions, since it would deny them that right. On the other hand, the legalization of abortion would not directly violate the consciences of Catholics, since they would not be legally compelled to have abortions. Catholic consciences would be infringed only indirectly, in that they would have to witness others' committing moral evil: this is excruciatingly difficult to accept where the particular moral evil consists of taking the lives of other human beings. But, in principle, despite this agonizing reality, I believe the result is the same as if a lesser sin were involved, viz., the consciences of Catholics are affected only indirectly.

Therefore legislation permitting abortion — or, what has the same effect, an absence of legislation prohibiting abortion — does not directly infringe any conscience. Those who believe abortion to be wrong are allowed by the law to live their own beliefs. Those who believe it to be right in appropriate circumstances are allowed to live by theirs. In this way, the law respects all consciences. This is the only kind of accommodation that in my opinion is ultimately consistent with democracy.

The law cannot fulfil its fundamental obligation to protect conscience from coercion in societies such as ours without permitting abortion. This is the price democracy exacts for the freedom it offers.

Catholics who see this result as a "concession" made by them or as a weak-kneed yielding to pressure are effectively invoking a "one-way democracy," which would hand them not only their freedom of conscience but their neighbours' as well. No such democracy exists, except, perhaps, in a tiny monolithic state like Ireland — nor could exist, where pluralism prevails. The Irish solution cannot be writ large, because Ireland cannot be taken as a prototype of the modern state — and, indeed, it should be noted that, even there, the natives are restless.[7]

So Catholics are not being asked to give up something they have or can have, but rather to recognize that democracy makes it impossible for them to enforce their morality by law — although, as I shall suggest, the Holy Spirit is not constrained by the law, but soars above it, leading us to more Christian ways of accomplishing the desired result.

CHAPTER 9

THE CHRISTIAN RECOGNITION OF ABORTION IN DEMOCRACY

So what should we Christians do after the law is decided against us? Should we become one-issue voters? Should we found our own political parties? Should we indulge in continuing demonstrations in the streets? Or should we bow to the massive majority?

What is fair ball for Christian dissenters who cannot reconcile themselves with a legal system that allows abortion? Obviously, they retain their normal democratic rights as citizens, to speak out individually and collectively.

A usual course for peaceful dissent in our society is to make use of civil disobedience, which I would define as a non-violent act of public protest which is either actually illegal or of contested legality. Its three primary elements are non-violence, publicity and illegality. It must be non-violent or it will degenerate into uncivil disobedience. It must be public, since its aim is to effect a change in the legal system through a combination of persuasion and coercion. It must break a minor law (for example, trespass) before it can actually be disobedience. There must also be a willingness, if not necessarily a positive desire, to accept the legal penalty for the disobedience.

There is, moreover, an overall requirement of purpose. Civil disobedience must thus be not only an act of protest but also an expression of a sense of justice based on conscience or a "higher law" theory.

In my view, civil disobedience which is true to its nature is a distinct contribution to democracy, driving the majority towards greater purity of action and policy. In its true nature it is coercive only in a psychological and not in a physically violent sense. But because civil disobedience requires such a fine balance of unstable elements in order to be true to its nature, it may move one way or the other, towards pacifism at one end or towards coercion at the other.

Pacifism is one of the most noble and most Christian movements of modern times, personified by Gandhi, Martin Luther King and Mother Theresa. It may well be called one of the "signs of the times" in the deepest theological sense of that expression.

To their everlasting shame, however, some anti-abortion protesters in the last few years have moved in the direction of coercion and violence rather than towards non-violence and pacifism. Tactics used have included the picketing of clinics and the homes of staff, the harassment of staff and those seeking abortions, the vandalization and bombing of abortion facilities, and, perhaps (since it is not known who did the shooting) even the shooting of abortionists. Indeed, the tendency seems to be for pro-life demonstrations at abortion clinics to become more and more violent. Such conduct is, of course, as destructive of democracy as is violence for any lesser motive.

The only current activist method that comes close to true civil disobedience in its pacifism is one used throughout the United States by Operation Rescue, which has involved courting arrest but refusing to provide one's name so that formal charges cannot be laid. Of course, this violates the requirement for true civil disobedience of accepting the assessed penalty when apprehended.[1]

At its best, civil disobedience may make a true contribution to democracy. As I wrote some years ago:[2]

> As a genuine example of the principle of persuasion, it is a variant and acceptable form of the political process which is at the heart of democracy. Democracy can ask no more than that its citizens, when for reasons of conscience they cannot obey a law, dissent respectfully and peacefully. If they also do so dramatically and persuasively, democracy is so much the richer.

However, even at its best, in my view it is not open to Christians to employ civil disobedience in the pro-life cause. The purpose of civil disobedience, after all, is specifically to bring about a change in the law, whereas, in the case of abortion, I believe the only permissible Christian goal must be to cause a change, not in the law, but in the attitudes behind it.

In my opinion, the democratic compact of which I have spoken allows Christians no choice but to accept the majority will, since at the same time their minority rights are protected. The law, being permissive, does not require Christians to engage in abortion. It lets all people follow their own consciences.

A law which permits abortion is not at all the standard of behaviour which Catholic Christians find acceptable for themselves, but, none of their rights is infringed merely because the law adopts a lower standard of permissible behaviour. Catholics can continue to follow their consciences with respect to abortion, while recognizing the right of the vast majority to legislate a different norm of conduct. Indeed, if we pose the opposite situation where pro-life forces were conceivably able to control Parliament long enough to pass a law prohibiting all abortion, this would, I believe, violate the democratic compact. By setting a higher standard of behaviour than the minority was able morally to accept, it would directly violate their rights. But in fact every sounding of public opinion consistently shows that they are in the majority, and we cannot prevent the majority of people in our society from doing what they believe is morally legitimate for them to do.

So the law and morality are, as is almost always the case, different, and the opposition between them, checkmated at the legal level, can best continue in the moral forum, as Christians continue to attempt to persuade others of the implications of the principle of life.

No Christian conscience can rest easy with an acceptance of the fact of abortion. It must bring great sadness to the heart. But it is not Christians who control Divine Providence. It is Divine Providence that, subject to the freedom of choice God allows us as rational beings, controls both present and future. Often the only option the Christian has is in the acceptance of the least bad option. That is why Christian morality always recognizes the principle of the lesser of evils.

It seems to me that the practical solution I suggest is demanded by the exigencies of democratic society, not only for the protection of minorities but also because there is in the last analysis no other way of resolving problems in a democracy. Unlike in a monarchy or a communist or fascist state, there is no person or group with the power to impose its will on the body politic. Only the majority of voters can determine the content of legislation. Of course, the majority in a democracy may be unstable, a possibility which constitutes a standing challenge to the minority to persuade it to change. Changing the *minds* of the majority is always a democratic option for a minority, provided that it proceeds by persuasion and not by coercion.

It was interesting to observe the recent recognition by the American Catholic bishops that a solution of the abortion issue might be found, not by treating it as an issue to be fought out politically, but through persuading the majority that abortion is morally wrong; in other words, by trying to persuade the majority to adopt a different moral code. Whether the most appropriate way to do this is through the $5 million public relations campaign the bishops adopted, through Madison Avenue techniques instead of the traditional Cathedral Way approach of prayer and preaching, is quite another question.

Christians' actions must in the last analysis be guided by the fact that their goal is not to change the law as such but rather to convert the majority to their point of view. As citizens, they retain their right to the exercise of all the democratic freedoms which are normally focussed on legislative change. But as Christians, they will not take advantage of these rights to militate for changes which they know they do not have the moral right to bring about, since such changes would not be respectful of others' consciences. However, provided that they can do so without infringing rights of conscience, I would agree with Professor Lisa Sowle Cahill that "misgivings about abortion" [on the part of non-Catholics] might be "the basis for an alliance in favour of social measures that will reduce abortion"[3] (for example, through persuasion rather than compulsion).

Catholics might also join with others in a campaign of non-abortion alternatives, which would seek to discourage rather than to forbid abortion. Such measures would obviously involve better social and economic conditions for family life, including perhaps initiatives such as Quebec's recent provision for heavy governmental bonuses to mothers having three or more children. The most efficacious non-abortion alternative would be, of course, effective contraception, a cause to which Catholics could bring immense strength, if their consciences would allow them to do so. As was suggested earlier, contraception may well be the key to combating abortion.

The state, too, has certain obligations. Its laws must ensure that those who do not believe in abortion do not have to participate in it in any way. I refer to Christian physicians and nurses for whom it is a matter of conscience not to assist in carrying out abortions. Public policy must ensure that the professional standing of such health care personnel is not affected in any adverse way by shunning such participation. Again, the operative principle is that of freedom of conscience.

Such exemptions for health care personnel are often referred to as "conscience clauses," and are defined by Professor Lynn D. Wardle as statutes or regulations "providing explicit protection for the rights of health care providers to decline to provide or participate in providing health care services that violate their religious or moral beliefs."[4] Such conscience clauses, at least as applied to abortion procedures, are general in the United States, though not in Canada. They are much more controversial when claimed by institutions than by individuals. In my view institutions that are sufficiently supported by public funds that they may be thought of as essentially public institutions have no right to invoke conscience clauses, but because there are so many different kinds of financing arrangements in existence it is desirable that the issue be settled by legislation rather than by the courts without guidance.

Under Charter influence Sunday closing legislation recognizes the necessity for statutory exemptions from work for employees who are other than Sunday observers on their days of observance. Chief Justice Dickson for Supreme Court of Canada in *R. v. Big M.Drug Mart Ltd.* has given a broad meaning to the freedom of religion:[5]

> *Freedom of Religion*
>
> A truly free society is one which can accommodate a wide variety of beliefs, diversity of tastes and pursuits, customs and codes of conduct. A free society is one which aims at equality with respect to the enjoyment of fundamental freedoms and I say this without any reliance upon s. 15 of the *Charter*. Freedom must surely be founded in respect for the inherent dignity and the inviolable rights of the human person. The essence of the concept of freedom of religion is the right to entertain such religious beliefs as a person chooses, the right to declare religious beliefs openly and without fear of hindrance or reprisal, and the right to manifest religious belief by worship and practice or by teaching and dissemination. But the concept means more than that.
>
> Freedom can primarily be characterized by the absence of coercion or constraint. If a person is compelled by the state or the will of another to a course of action or inaction which he would not otherwise have chosen, he is not acting of his own volition and he cannot be said to be truly free. One of the major purposes of the *Charter* is to protect, within reason, from compulsion or restraint. Coercion includes not only such blatant forms of compulsion as direct commands to act or refrain from acting on pain of sanction, coercion includes indirect forms of control which determine or limit alternative courses of conduct available to others. Freedom in a broad sense embraces both the absence of coercion and constraint, and the right to manifest beliefs and practices. Freedom means that, subject to such limitations as are necessary to protect public safety, order, health, or morals or the fundamental rights and freedoms of others, no one is to be forced to act in a way contrary to his beliefs or his conscience.

Full freedom is here said to include not only the absence of coercion or constraint, but also the right to manifest beliefs and practices; in other words, it is positive as well as negative. It must at least be obvious that with respect to its primary instance of the absence of coercion it must be given very full scope. Whether or not, therefore, the state were under a legally enforceable obligation affirmatively to protect the rights of Christian health professionals not to participate in abortions, the democratic compact of which I have spoken would surely require it to do so. That would include even existing situations in Canada where there is no criminal legislation at all respecting abortion. The effect of such an absence of legislation is to protect the consciences of those who demand choice. In such circumstances the state retains the equal obligation to protect the consciences of those opposed to abortion by ensuring that they shall not be constrained to participate in it. This general governmental obligation is in no way lessened by the fact that, because of a federal-provincial division of legislative power, the obligation to protect dissenters may rest on a provincial legislature, rather than on the federal parliament which chose not to enact abortion legislation. The democratic compact must be fulfilled by whatever government has the legislative power to do so.

Because the issue sometimes arises in practice, I should for the sake of completeness deal also with the position of Christian police officers ordered to restrain pro-life supporters who may be protesting in an unruly fashion at an abortion clinic. To my mind, there is no similarity between their position and that of health professionals required to assist in abortions. The duty of police officers has nothing whatever to do with abortion, or indeed with the "cause" of any demonstration. If demonstrators violate the law by their actions (perhaps by way of civil disobedience), the law — and those sworn to uphold it — must deal with those actions as effectively as they can. Police officers' role is to keep the peace, and Christian officers who do not fulfil their sworn duties to do so, out of sympathy for whatever cause, should expect the usual disciplinary result.

In addition to its responsibility towards dissenting health professionals, the state retains its duty to protect the rights of all its citizens to exercise their normal democratic freedoms, including the right to conduct peaceful demonstrations against permissive abortion policies. The Ontario Government was accordingly rebuffed in an attempt to enjoin such picketing within 500 feet of twenty-two locations. Nevertheless, Adams J., while finding no case for limits on hospital picketing, allowed an exclusion zone of 500 feet only for picketing near the homes of nine physicians; for abortion clinics, the exclusion zone established was sixty feet in two cases, and thirty feet in another, as contrasted with the thirty-six-foot buffer zone upheld in the United States for an abortion clinic.[6]

The democratic compact, therefore, cuts both ways. On the one hand, it binds Christians not to try to change the abortion laws in ways violative of others' freedom of conscience. On the other, it must protect Christians in the exercise of their freedom not to aid and abet abortion.

CHAPTER 10

EUTHANASIA AND SUICIDE

This is a book on abortion, not on moral problems in general. Nevertheless, since the "life issue" at the end of a normal life span is becoming equally a matter of public debate as that at the beginning, intellectual completeness, to say nothing of intellectual honesty, compels me to face the implications of the conscience principle here elaborated at least for the more obvious issues with respect to euthanasia and suicide.

Euthanasia is very much more complex, both morally and legally, than abortion. In fact, there is no single issue of euthanasia, but a congeries of related problems and questions.[1]

As background on the morals side, for Catholics we can begin with the 1980 Declaration on Euthanasia by the Sacred Congregation for the Doctrine of the Faith.[2] The remote principles are easy enough to state: (1) taking someone else's life is a crime of the utmost gravity; (2) taking one's own life is equally as wrong as murder, since it is a rejection of God's sovereignty over our lives, as well as a denial of the natural instinct to live. Nevertheless, the use of medicines capable of alleviating or suppressing pain is permissible, even though they may cause as a secondary effect semi-consciousness and reduced lucidity — the only limitation is that painkillers that cause unconsciousness must not be used to prevent a person from preparing to "meet God" and from satisfying family obligations.

Catholic moralists have always made use of the distinction between ordinary and extraordinary means — with the advances in medicine and medical technology in which the extraordinary tends to become the ordinary, the distinction might best be interpreted as one between proportionate and disproportionate means. Thus ordinary and proportionate means to safeguard life are morally required to be taken, whereas extraordinary and disproportionate means are not. The Declaration concludes with the counsel that:[3]

> When inevitable death is imminent in spite of the means used, it is permitted in conscience to take the decision to refuse forms of treatment that would only secure a precarious and burdensome prolongation of life, so long as the normal care due the sick person in similar cases is not interrupted.

As a commentary on end-of-life issues, the bishops of Ireland issued a pastoral letter in 1975 in which they made the point that "giving drugs to lessen pain is totally different from giving a lethal overdose of drugs to end life."[4] They also found the ending of the artificial prolongation of life justified when it could not be said to be properly life-supporting:[5]

> 66. A very real problem arises when artificial measures of resuscitation and life-support become death-delaying rather than properly life-supporting ... Such medicine could be an assault on human dignity and on man's right to a dignified death. There is clearly no moral obligation to keep a body breathing and biologically alive after irreversible brain death has occurred. It is not euthanasia to decline the use of such means or even to discontinue them when it is clear that they are only death delaying.

Occasional comments of Catholic theologians make it clear that, for the plug to be pulled on disproportionate means of maintaining life, it is not regarded as necessary that the patient personally make the decision to discontinue treatment. Indeed, the patient may be in a persistent vegetative state (PVS), and the only moral issue may be who will have the right to make the decision.[6] In my own view, such a decision to end treatment cannot extend to nutrition and hydration, which to my mind are ordinary and proportionate means of maintaining life.

It must also be remarked that despite its strong insistence on the immorality of suicide, the Church has accepted with remarkable equanimity the removal of suicide and attempted suicide from the criminal legislation of almost every Western country in the 1960s and 1970s. I can assume only that this is a recognition that this is an area of personal morality which is not the law's business because it is outside the common good of society. (It should be noted, however, that most jurisdictions have retained aiding or assisting suicide as a criminal offence.) Nevertheless, this is an area in which morality, at least as interpreted by the Church, establishes a higher standard than the law.

I should add that in Catholic theology the term "euthanasia" is used only pejoratively. When a means of death is unacceptable, it is called euthanasia. When it is regarded as licit, it is distinguished from euthanasia.

The first controversy, therefore, is over how euthanasia should be defined. The *Shorter Oxford English Dictionary* (Third Edition, 1984) says simply that it is the action of inducing a quiet and easy death. Professor Ronald Dworkin in *Life's Dominion* has recently defined it as "deliberately killing a person *out of kindness.*" (Emphasis added.) I find it questionable thus to include in the definition that the act is always performed for the benefit of the person killed. Not only may the reasons for euthanasia be abstractly social rather than personally benevolent, but the person affected might have been opposed if capable of being consulted. Of course, this is far from Professor Dworkin's intention, but the word "euthanasia" may bear that meaning.

We do not need to go to Nazi Germany to find advocates of the notion that the old and the infirm, the deformed and the incurable should be left to die by the wayside of life. This was Herbert Spencer's theory of natural selection before it was Adolf Hitler's policy.

We are not yet so far from *Buck* v. *Bell* (1927), when the U.S. Supreme Court upheld the sterilization of mental defectives in the harsh words of the usually judicious and otherwise admired Mr. Justice Holmes:[7]

> The principle that sustains compulsory vaccination is broad enough to cover cutting the Fallopian tubes. Three generations of imbeciles are enough.

There is little sympathy with such a hard-boiled approach in this age of greater awareness of civil liberties, but analogous views are not entirely absent from our society. A recent poll in France, for instance, indicated that 42 percent of its respondents (women of child-bearing age) were in favour of putting to death newly born seriously malformed infants, with 20 percent of the sample undecided.[8] The study apparently did not attempt to measure to what extent such a preference was motivated by sympathy for the condition of the infants and to what extent it was out of sympathy for the burden of care on the parents.

Hence a basic distinction must be made between voluntary and involuntary euthanasia, depending on whether the victim consents to the act (or consent can be readily implied from the circumstances) or death is imposed on the victim with neither actual nor implied consent. The Irish bishops purport to find a great deal of support for involuntary euthanasia. They write: "It is obvious, and is admitted even by some euthanasiasts themselves, that an even stronger case can be made for people incapable of choice (such as mentally handicapped or incurably mentally ill people) than can be made for so-called voluntary euthanasia."[9] Personally, I do not yet find this to be a significant current of our times. Nevertheless, my own language usage will always qualify the word "euthanasia," so that we know exactly what we are dealing with, or avoid it entirely in favour of traditional terms such as "suicide" — or, where appropriate, "assisted suicide."

No doubt there are large numbers of cases of voluntary euthanasia in the guise of treatment or the cessation of treatment. Allegedly, such deaths occur every day in Canada but are kept secret, and a recent Canadian Medical Association survey has shown that 60 percent of physicians in Canada are in favour of legalizing some form of euthanasia and physician-assisted suicide,[10] although the association is officially on record to the contrary.

The kinds of cases referred to by the physicians' survey are obviously cases of active euthanasia, in which the attending physician takes steps directly and purposefully (with consent) to end the patient's life, rather than merely the cessation of treatment. The Law Reform Commission of Canada stated in its 1983 report that "the legalization of [active] euthanasia is unacceptable to the Commission because it would indirectly condone murder, because it would be open to serious abuses, and because it appears to be morally unacceptable to the majority of the Canadian people."[11] (The third reason is not so clearly correct ten years later.) The Commission therefore recommended that Parliament retain section 241 in the Canadian Criminal Code. It reads as follows:

> 241. Everyone who
> (a) counsels ... a person to commit suicide, or
> (b) aids or abets a person to commit suicide,
> whether suicide ensues or not, is guilty of an indictable offence and liable to imprisonment for a term not exceeding fourteen years.

More than half of the American states have similar legislation.

❦

Even with the aid of many distinctions, the difficulty of decision making in this area is well illustrated by recent decisions of the ultimate courts in the United States, Great Britain and Canada. In *Cruzan* v. *Director, Missouri Department of Health*[12] (the Nancy Cruzan case) the Supreme Court of the United States divided 5 to 4 on a "right to die" issue concerning a PVS automobile accident victim. The thirty-year-old woman was not terminably ill and might live another thirty years. Her respiration and circulation were not artificially maintained, but she had no cognitive or reflexive ability to swallow food or water to maintain her daily essential needs.

The state trial court held that a person in her condition had a fundamental right under both state and federal constitutions to refuse or terminate death-prolonging procedures, and it found that at the age of twenty-five the victim had expressed the view in conversation with a housemate friend that, if sick or injured, she would not wish to continue her life unless she could live at least "halfway normally."

The Supreme Court of Missouri reversed by a divided vote, recognizing a right to refuse treatment embodied in the common-law doctrine of informed consent, where such consent can be given, but refusing to accept a broad right of privacy which would justify a person's guardians to refuse medical treatment in these circumstances. In the light of a state policy strongly favouring the preservation of life, embodied in the state's "living will" legislation, it held that the patient's statements to her roommate regarding her desire to live or die in certain circumstances were an unreliable indication of her intent, and that her parents could not assume her choice in the absence of the formalities required by the state's living will law. The court expressed the view that "broad policy questions bearing on life and death are more properly addressed by representative assemblies" than by courts.

The issue as argued before the U.S. Supreme Court was whether the victim had a constitutional right to require the hospital to withdraw life-sustaining treatment. The majority of the court acknowledged that under the due process clause of the Fourteenth Amendment a *competent* person has a constitutionally protected liberty interest in refusing unwanted medical assistance, and was prepared to assume for purposes of this case that this liberty interest for a competent person extends even to refusing lifesaving hydration and nutrition. Its difference with the minority arose over whether an incompetent person possessed the same rights as a competent one in this respect.

Justice Brennan, in dissent, took the position that the due process clause permitted a state to ensure only that a person making the decision to refuse medical treatment on behalf of an incompetent person be one that person would have selected, and to exclude from consideration anyone having improper motives. Otherwise, a state must either repose the choice with the person the patient would most likely have chosen as proxy or leave the decision to the patient's family. He raised the question:[13]

> Is there any reason to suppose that a State is *more* likely to make the choice the patient would have made than someone who knows the patient intimately? To ask this question is to answer it. As the New Jersey Supreme Court observed: "Family members are best qualified to make substituted judgments for incompetent patients not only because of their

peculiar grasp of the patient's approach to life, but also because of their special bonds with him or her ... It is ... they who treat the patient as a person, rather than a symbol of a cause ..." The State, in contrast, is a stranger to the patient.

Justice Scalia, concurring with the majority opinion, summed up the dissenters' position this way:[14]

> It seems to me ... that Justice Brennan's position ultimately rests upon the proposition that it is none of the State's business if a person wants to commit suicide. Justice Stevens is explicit on the point: "choices about death touch the core of liberty ... [N]ot much may be said with confidence about death unless it is said from faith, and that alone is reason enough to protect the freedom to conform choices about death to individual conscience."

The majority held that due process did not forbid a state from requiring that evidence of an incompetent person's wishes be proved by clear and convincing evidence, and that the Missouri Supreme Court did not commit constitutional error in deciding that the evidence did not meet that standard. Justice O'Connor, concurring, wanted it understood that there may well be a constitutional requirement that states must implement the decisions of a duly appointed surrogate, but that it was a matter for future determination.

✦

The case before the British House of Lords, *Airedale NHS Trust* v. *Bland* (the *Tony Bland* case) was very similar to the *Nancy Cruzan* case, but led to a different result. Because of an accident at a sporting event, a teenaged male fell into a PVS in which he had continued for over three years. The issue was whether artificial feedings and antibiotic drugs might lawfully be withheld from the patient when it was known that if this were done the patient would die shortly thereafter. The principal speech in the House was read by Lord Goff of Chieveley.

In Lord Goff's view the fundamental principle of the sanctity of human life must yield to the principle of self-determination, so that "if an adult patient of sound mind refuses, however unreasonably, to consent to treatment or care by which his life would or might be prolonged, the doctors responsible for his care must give effect to his wishes, even though they do not consider it in his best interests to do so."[15] In the case where patients have left no prior indication of their wishes and are not in a condition to say whether or not they accept treatment or care, "there is nevertheless no absolute obligation upon the doctor who has the patient in his care to prolong his life, regardless of the circumstances."[16]

Lord Goff points out that the law draws a crucial distinction between cases of non-continuance of treatment or care and those where the physician might administer a lethal drug, actively to bring life to an end:[17]

> But it is not lawful for a doctor to administer a drug to his patient to bring about his death, even though that course is prompted by a humanitarian desire to end his suffering, however great that suffering may be .... So to act is to cross the Rubicon which runs between on the one hand the care of the living patient and on the other hand euthanasia — actively causing his death to avoid or to end his suffering. Euthanasia is not lawful at common law. It is of course well known that there are many responsible members of our society who believe that euthanasia should be made lawful; but that result could, I believe, only be achieved by legislation which expresses the democratic will that so fundamental a change should be made in our law, and can, if enacted, ensure that such legalised killing can only be carried out subject to appropriate supervision and control.

The "Rubicon" distinction made by Lord Goff is the one I have already referred to between active euthanasia and the cessation of treatment. As Lord Goff emphasizes, it is only actively causing death which is normally considered euthanasia.

The Court in this case did not feel that it had to deal with the absence of consent as an issue because the artificial feeding and the antibiotics the patient was receiving were considered by it to be extraordinary means of care, which might therefore be discontinued:[18]

> In the present case it is proposed that the doctors should be entitled to discontinue both the artificial feeding of Anthony and the use of antibiotics. It is plain from the evidence that Anthony, in his present condition, is very prone to infection and that, over some necessarily uncertain but not very long period of time, he will succumb to infection which, if unchecked, will spread and cause his death. But the effect

of discontinuing the artificial feeding will be that he will inevitably die within one or two weeks.

Objection can be made to the latter course of action on the ground that Anthony will thereby be starved to death, and that this would constitute a breach of the duty to feed him which must form an essential part of the duty which every person owes to another in his care. But here again it is necessary to analyze precisely what this means in the case of Anthony. Anthony is not merely incapable of feeding himself. He is incapable of swallowing, and therefore of eating or drinking in the normal sense of those words. There is overwhelming evidence that, in the medical profession, artificial feeding is regarded as a form of medical treatment; and, even if it is not strictly medical treatment, it must form part of the medical care of the patient. Indeed, the function of artificial feeding in the case of Anthony, by means of a nasogastric tube, is to provide a form of life support analogous to that provided by a ventilator which artificially breathes air in and out of the lungs of a patient incapable of breathing normally, thereby enabling oxygen to reach the bloodstream. The same principles must apply in either case when the question is asked whether the doctor in charge may lawfully discontinue the life-sustaining treatment or care; and, if in either case the treatment is futile in the sense I have described, it can properly be concluded that it is no longer in the best interests of the patient to continue it. It is true that, in the case of discontinuance of artificial feeding, it can be said that the patient will as a result starve to death; and this may bring before our eyes the vision of an ordinary person slowly dying of hunger, and suffering all the pain and distress associated with such a death. But here it is clear from the evidence that no such pain or distress will be suffered by Anthony, who can feel nothing at all. Furthermore, we are told that the outward symptoms of dying in such a way, which might otherwise cause distress to the nurses who care for him or to members of his family who visit him, can be suppressed by means of sedatives. In these circumstances, I can see no ground in the present case for refusing the declarations applied for simply because the course of action proposed involves the discontinuance of artificial feeding.

The unanimous decision of the House of Lords in Tony Bland's case was therefore similar to that of the minority in Nancy Cruzan's case, though based entirely on common-law principles rather than on the Bill of Rights basis of Justices Brennan and Stevens.

※◎◎※

The Canadian case, *Rodriguez* v. *Attorney General of Canada* (the *Sue Rodriguez* case), had to do with a competent but terminally ill woman who, because of physical disability, would need assistance in committing suicide. The patient was a forty-two-year-old woman terminally ill with amyotrophic lateral sclerosis (AML), commonly known as Lou Gehrig's disease. AML is an incurable, progressive disease affecting the nervous system, which usually causes death within three years after diagnosis. It causes difficulties with speech, chewing and swallowing, with death ultimately resulting from starvation or choking. The particular patient, Sue Rodriguez, did not want to die so long as she still had the capacity to enjoy life, and proposed to have a physician install an intravenous device containing an effective agent *which she could activate to end her life* by use of a switch at a time of her own choosing. She sought a declaration that provisions of the Criminal Code were invalid to the extent that they prohibit a terminally ill person from committing physician-assisted suicide. The trial judge dismissed her application, and the British Columbia Court of Appeal dismissed her appeal on a 2 to 1 division.[19]

In the Supreme Court of Canada the appeal was rejected on a 5 to 4 vote.[20] The principal issue was over the application of section 7 of the Charter with its guarantee of "the right to life, liberty and security of the person and the right not to be deprived thereof except in accordance with the principles of fundamental justice."

Justice Sopinka for the majority admitted that the prohibition in subsection 241(b) of the Criminal Code of aiding or abetting the commission of suicide engaged the security of the person in section 7, since that security encompasses notions of personal autonomy in relation to physical and psychological integrity, and basic human dignity. However, in the majority's view, any resulting impingement on the security of the person (or any other section 7 liberty) could not be said on the facts to be contrary to the principles of fundamental justice.

The principles of fundamental justice must be not only fundamental to our notion of justice and identifiable with some precision, Justice Sopinka said, but they must also be legal principles, and represent a fair balance between the interests of the state and those of the individual. The respect for human dignity, although an underlying principle of our society, is not a principle of fundamental justice in the sense of section 7.

In particular, since it is common ground that subsection 241(b) is generally valid, and that the issue is only whether the legislation is over-inclusive and arbitrary as not excluding those who are terminally ill (while mentally competent) but who cannot commit suicide on their own, the defining of the state's interest requires a consideration of the legal tradition and societal beliefs represented by the prohibition. Such a review leads both in law and society to a rejection of the active assistance of a third party:[21]

> The basis for this refusal is twofold it seems — first, the active participation by one individual in the death of another is intrinsically morally and legally wrong, and second, there is no certainty that abuses can be prevented by anything less than a complete prohibition. Creating an exception for the terminally ill might therefore frustrate the purpose of the legislation of protecting the vulnerable because adequate guidelines to control abuse are difficult or impossible to develop.

Moreover, "a blanket prohibition on assisted suicide similar to that in s. 241 is the norm among Western democracies, and such a prohibition has never been adjudged to be unconstitutional or contrary to fundamental human rights."[22]

The right of patients to refuse or discontinue treatment, even where death will result, is well established at common law,[23] but in the majority's view may be distinguished on the basis of the passive-active distinction: in the case of mere withdrawal of treatment, the death is "natural," whereas in the case of active intervention, death results directly from the human action taken.

Justice Beverley McLachlin for the minority took the point that the denial to the appellant of a right available to others cannot be justified, since the potential for abuse can be adequately guarded against. In her view this case should be decided on the same basis on which the abortion question was resolved in R. v. Morgentaler No. 2 in 1988 [24] and for the same reasons:[25]

> In my view, the reasoning of the majority in R. v. Morgentaler ... is dispositive of the issues on this appeal. In the present case, Parliament has put into force a legislative scheme which does not bar suicide but criminalizes the act of assisting suicide. The effect of this is to deny to some people the choice of ending their lives solely because they are physically unable to do so. This deprives Sue Rodriguez of her security of the person (the right to make decisions concern-

ing her own body, which affect only her own body) in a way that offends the principles of fundamental justice (thereby violating s. 7 of the *Charter*). The violation cannot be saved under s. 1. This is precisely the logic which led the majority of this Court to strike down the abortion provisions of the *Criminal Code* in *Morgentaler*. In that case, Parliament had set up a scheme authorizing therapeutic abortion. The effect of the provisions was in fact to deny or delay therapeutic abortions to some women. This was held to violate s. 7 because it deprived some women of the right to deal with their own bodies as they chose thereby infringing their security of the person, in a manner which did not comport with the principles of fundamental justice. Parliament could not advance an interest capable of justifying this arbitrary legislative scheme, and, accordingly the law was not saved under s. 11 of the *Charter*.

With respect to the argument of possible abuse of legislative tolerance of assisted suicide, Justice McLachlin commented that "Sue Rodriguez is asked to bear the burden of the chance that other people in other situations may act criminally to kill others or improperly sway them to suicide. She is asked to serve as a scapegoat."[26]

As to the majority's view that active participation by one individual in the death of another is intrinsically morally and legally wrong, she stated:[27]

[T]here is no absolute rule that causing or assisting in the death of another is criminally wrong ... The law has long recognized that if there is a valid justification for bringing about someone's death, the person who does so will not be held criminally responsible. In the case of Sue Rodriguez, there is arguably such a justification — the justification of giving her the capacity to end her life which able-bodied people have as a matter of course, and the justification of her clear consent and desire to end her life at a time when, in her view, it makes no sense to continue living it.

Chief Justice Lamer, also in the minority, would have decided the issue for Rodriguez on the basis of the equality provisions of s. 15 rather than under the fundamental justice notion of s. 7 (Cory J. agreed with both McLachlin J. and Lamer C.J.C.). The minority judges generally agreed with Lamer C.J.C.'s analysis of the remedy (although McLachlin J. noted that she was "not convinced that some of the conditions laid down by his guidelines are essential"):[28] that a declaration of constitutional invalidity should be made against s. 241 (*b*) of the Criminal Code, but only after a year from the date of judgment so as to give Parliament long enough to address the issue, but that in the meantime Rodriguez and any others in a similar position could seek a constitutional exemption by way of application to a superior court, with certification by two physicians as to mental competence and voluntariness, on notice to the regional coroner, and *that the act of causing the death of the applicant must be that of the applicant and not of anyone else* (although this latter condition, here proposed by the applicant herself, was left open for future judicial consideration).[29]

In the sequel, Sue Rodriguez took her own life on 12 February 1994, apparently with the aid of a thus-far-nameless physician. At the time of writing, no charges had been laid.

<hr/>

The most recent development has been the Report of the Select Committee of the House of Lords on Medical Ethics (The Walton Report),[30] released in the United Kingdom on 17 February 1994. The Select Committee was unanimous in coming to the view that the traditional prohibition of intentional killing has to prevail. The Walton Report said:[31]

> 236. The right to refuse treatment is far removed from the right to request assistance in dying. We spent a long time considering the very strongly held and sincerely expressed views of those witnesses who advocated voluntary euthanasia ...

> 237. Ultimately, however, we do not believe that those arguments are sufficient reason to weaken society's prohibition on intentional killing. *That prohibition is the cornerstone of law and of social relationships. It protects each one of us impartially, embodying the belief that all are equal* ... We believe that the issue of euthanasia is one in which the interest of the individual cannot be separated from the interest of society as a whole. (emphasis mine)

The Committee seems to have been principally influenced by the danger of abuse, particularly of undue pressure on vulnerable people:[32]

238. One reason for this conclusion is that we do not think it is possible to set secure limits on voluntary euthanasia ... It would be next to impossible to ensure that all acts of euthanasia were truly voluntary, and that any liberalisation of the law was not abused. Moreover to create an exception to the general prohibition of intentional killing would inevitably open the way to its further erosion whether by design, by inadvertence, or by the human tendency to test the limits of any regulation ...

239. *We are also concerned that vulnerable people — the elderly, lonely, sick or distressed — would feel pressure, whether real or imagined, to request early death ...*

241. Furthermore, there is good evidence that, through the outstanding achievements of those who work in the field of palliative care, the pain and distress of terminal illness can be adequately relieved in the vast majority of cases. (emphasis mine)

A principal consequence of a rejection of assisted suicide is, of course, the necessity to provide adequate care for the dying. In the words of the Walton Report, "the rejection of euthanasia as an option for the individual, in the interest of our wider social good, entails a compelling social responsibility to care adequately for those who are elderly, dying or disabled."[33]

As I have said, there is a complex of issues with respect to the end of life. No single case will subsume them all. No single principle will resolve them all. My modest purpose is only to delineate the effect of the conscience principle.

With respect to the purest cases of conscientious self-determination, viz., *un*assisted suicide and attempted suicide, the question has already been decided in favour of conscience by the removal of these cases from the law.

With respect to assisted suicide in terminal cases, however, common-law courts have so far been unable to accept that physicians actively and directly cause death or cooperate in it (as in the Netherlands) by the provision of drugs or devices which are subsequently self-activated by the patients. Assisting in suicide seems also to go against the moral instincts of physicians themselves — a moral repugnance which one can understand.

Nevertheless, at the level of law, I am unable to distinguish such accommodation of the consciences of terminal patients by physicians in assisted suicide from their role in the carrying out of abortions. In each case, the determining factor is the patient's free exercise of conscience, and the physician's role is only that of a means to that end. Being used as a means to such an end may be morally wrong, since the physician would be immediately cooperating in the suicide, but I cannot see that it should have any more legal significance in one case than in the other. At law, it would seem that the physician should be merely the executor of the patients' will.

Given that suicide itself is not illegal, a starting point that has now become general in the West, it seems entirely illogical to me that aiding or abetting it should be an offence. I cannot distinguish this situation from that of Nancy B., where a patient suffering from the Guillain-Barré syndrome was herself unable to turn off her respirator and obtained an order compelling her hospital and physician to do so.[34] Of course, it would be incumbent on the law to ensure that assisted suicide is not used as a cloak either for murder, or for pressuring "unwanted people" into suicide, and the very complexity of the remedy proposed by Chief Justice Lamer makes clear the desirability that the matter be legislatively rather than judicially resolved.

However, my own concern about the possibility of undue pressure on the vulnerable leads me to the conclusion that the law should permit assisted suicide only to the extent of assistance in the preparation of the means, and that the actual act of causing death must be that of the would-be suicide alone. I do not see this safeguard as limiting an absolute right of negative conscience so much as ensuring that the act involved is that of the would-be suicide's own conscience, and not that of some omniscient external force. The recent revelation in the Report of the New York State Task Force on Life and the Law[35] that in the Netherlands nearly one-third of physician-assisted deaths occurred without an explicit written request, as required by the law there, and that nearly 1 percent of these were clearly non-consent euthanasia decided upon by the physician stands as an object lesson for other countries. *Hence, in my view assisted suicide should be allowed by law only to the extent that it is tantamount to unassisted suicide.* (emphasis added)

Also I would repeat that, in the limited circumstances where it should be permitted by law, the issue of assisted suicide is better decided in favour of the patient under subsection 2(a), the Charter's freedom-of-conscience provision, rather than by virtue of section 7.

The priority of the freedom of conscience also throws light on the other major issues. Since conscience requires awareness, it finds no expression in the absence of consent, and certainly none in a case where the person is in a persistent vegetative state. Of course, where the situation is one of withdrawal of extraordinary means of life-maintenance, other principles operate to allow such a withdrawal. But this is not the case with the cessation of ordinary means of treatment. I am therefore not in agreement with the House of Lords in the *Tony Bland* case (since I cannot see that the means involved were extraordinary), nor with the minority in the *Nancy Cruzan* case. In fact, I would go even further than the majority in *Cruzan* to argue that where there is no express consent (at the very least through a living will), there should not be any termination of *ordinary* medical care.

Since food is one of the basic human necessities, I disagree with the *Tony Bland* result that the continuance of a food supply, where the patient cannot swallow, can be somehow thought of as an unusual medical treatment, merely because it involves the use of a nasogastric tube. The effect of the tube's removal is the sheer starvation of the patient, even if with the House of Lords our sensibilities are spared, through the use of sedatives, from seeing the outward symptoms of dying.[36]

The Walton Committee could not reach agreement on the cessation of nutrition and hydration in the *Bland* case, but did agree that "it might well have been decided long before application was made to the court that treatment with antibiotics was inappropriate, given that recovery from the inevitable complication of infection could add nothing to his well-being as a person."[37] I can agree that such a course would have been legally appropriate.

As in the case of abortion, the conscience principle, not morality, should determine what the law should be. Conscience, however, has only limited application in this area, since so many cases have to do with unconscious people. Only in the specific circumstances of Sue Rodriguez, where the act of suicide is to be committed by the patient herself, should the law countenance it on the basis of conscience.

PART THREE

CHRISTIANITY IN ACTION

CHAPTER 11

THE FALLACY OF THE LAW AS IDOL

The relationship between law and morals is a multifaceted one that cannot be simply stated. However, in my view Fr. Sertillanges's definition of morals has never been bettered: "the science of what a man ought to be by reason of what he is."[1]

For me the standard of morals and the moral life is right reason. A reasonable act, by the very fact that it is reasonable, is moral. Morals come from within the person, not from the outside. As I put it some decades ago:[2]

> Of course God has created man and his nature and so is in this indirect sense the author of morals. Hence God in a sense imposes morality upon man, but not by legislating it. He imposes it only by, as it were, imposing upon man his nature. God makes man and man makes morality — or rather finds morality, in his own nature and in other natures.

The Church may, of course, also be of considerable assistance to Christians in interpreting moral principles, but it cannot speak with infallible authority about matters that are not contained in the Word of God, and, as we saw in chapter 1 with respect to contraception and other historical issues, it is sometimes for a time even in error in its official teaching on what may be deduced from natural law, which is not a matter for defined dogma — in such cases the consensus of the faithful may stand as the clearest witness of Christian morals.

I have emphasized throughout that law and morals are distinct and separate in concept. They are not, however, totally independent in operation, but have a certain interrelationship, which is complicated to express because it involves a complex reality. In the introduction I made it clear that they do not simply incorporate each other, but I also stated that criminal law is dependent on morality for its legitimacy and acceptance.

Although every human act in the concrete must, I believe, be either good or bad (depending on the practical reason or conscience of the person), human acts taken generically are of three kinds, viz., generically good, generically evil, and generically indifferent. This is the source of the common law's distinction between *mala in se* (acts which are generically or intrinsically evil) and those which are merely *mala prohibita*, taking their moral character in the concrete not from their natures but from their circumstances. Most ordinary human acts are of this third kind, and generally speaking this realm of what is neither morally good nor morally bad but morally permissible is the domain of human positive law.

With respect to acts which have an intrinsic morality (such as those forbidden by the second table of the Decalogue), morals has a substantive effect upon positive law, in that the moral prohibition of such acts can be described as the source of positive law, whereas with respect to morally neutral acts their effect can be at most adjectival or procedural.

But there is not only a penetration of morals into law. There is a mutual interpenetration in that, once a legislature has decided what the law shall be in a morally neutral area, what was previously morally neutral becomes morally required.

To take a concrete example, while the moral law may be said to require that the driver of a motor vehicle drive so as not to imperil the lives or limbs of others, stop signs and traffic lights and driving on the right (in British-influenced countries, on the left) are legislative determinations in a morally neutral area. Once they are legislated, however, they become, secondarily, moral rules, so that people become morally obligated to obey the legislated rules of the road — unless relieved in some individual circumstances by the application of *epikeia*, as suggested in chapter 1. As I have previously written, "once the means have been determined by the superior wisdom of the legislator, the citizens must accept them as *the* ways of achieving the common good, or else the very purpose of the legislator's authority will be frustrated."[3] Such legislated morality is, of course, a secondary and derived kind of moral obligation.

Although, as I have said, law for the most part operates in the realm of otherwise generic moral neutrality, in a very important respect it has need of the support of morals, that is, with regard to the actual behaviour of the citizen body. Particularly in the field of criminal law, it is because of the coincidence of legal rules with moral principles that good order exists in most bodies politic. Legal sanctions alone, for all their coerciveness, are not enough to guarantee obedience to law.

This underpinning of the legal order by the moral is of crucial importance to law. In fact, in my opinion the essential emptiness of the positivist theory of law, which bases law purely upon the command of the sovereign and so totally divorces it from morals, is shown most clearly by the fact that it has logically to deny itself this support from the people's moral roots. As I have written:[4]

> It is not morality that is destroyed by the [positivist] sep-
> aration of law and morals; what is destroyed is ultimately the
> law itself, for the theory of separation removes the *raison
> d'être* and ground of law, and in doing so robs it of its obliga-
> tion, of its power of inducing assent and conformity.

The beneficent effect of morals on law is nowhere better seen than in relation to racial and other human rights issues. The greatest importance of the Supreme Court decision, *Brown* v. *Board of Education*,[5] in the United States was not its legal reversal of a generations-old legal principle as to "separate but equal" schools, although that was a great achievement in itself. Rather, to my mind its larger significance results from the way it was able to reach back to Americans' moral consciousness and to give a specifically moral impetus to social reform, fostered in large part by Martin Luther King, who, it must not be forgotten, was a man of high religious motivation and principle. The race movement in the United States has not been law-driven, although it has marked its progress by legal landmarks. Rather, it has been conscience-driven. It would probably not be too much to say that *Brown* v. *Board of Education* has revolutionized American society, and it has done so by harnessing the inherent morality of the American people.

For the most part, however, the law is not in such direct communion with morals. Its usual level, as we saw in earlier chapters, is much below that of morals, its usual technique being to establish a least-common-denominator approach to behaviour, well below that which Christians set for themselves as their own standard of conduct.

※

What, then, about the symbolic aspect of the law? In an era when constitutional controversies have filled the front pages of Canadian newspapers, no one could dispute that symbolism often is as important as factual reality. The law, it may well be said, symbolizes for many in our society what is morally, and not just legally, right. But is this what law generally does? Does the law generally not rather, as I have suggested, connote and symbolize only the *minimum* of socially permissible behaviour?

For clarification, let us look at some examples. In the days before manufacturers' liability to consumers for defects in products was as fully established as now, would any Christian moralist have maintained that a manufacturer's total responsibility to produce an acceptable product was measured only by the letter of the law? Or what about the question of marital fidelity? Adultery is no longer a crime in most jurisdictions today, but does that mean that a Christian judgment as to the morality of extramarital sexual relations should merely echo that of the law? Is the absence of a legal prohibition to be taken as moral exoneration? I cannot imagine that any Christian moralist would so argue.

What is it, then, about the law that makes moralists want to use it? Is it merely that it facilitates and simplifies the Church's task? Certainly it can have that effect, and so enable the Church merely to point to the fact of the law to establish the norm of morality.

That may possibly be a factor in the equation, but I believe that the real reason goes deeper. The law, I venture even as a lawyer to say, has become, not an ideal, but an idol, an idol possessing bountiful powers of seduction. In a different context Professor Valerie Kerruish has recently criticized "rights fetishism," which she identifies with "the irrational reverencing of a human artefact."[6]

There may be many reasons for this situation, but in my view the principal one is the omnipresence and seeming omnipotence of the state. Today, in the world beyond people's private lives it is perhaps the most prominent reality. Its stature has been augmented in recent times by its role in bringing about increased freedom for minorities, beginning with the struggle for racial equality we have observed in the United States and continuing with the cause of women's rights and homosexual rights. To some extent — and understandably — these minorities tend to define themselves in terms of their status as recognized in the law, and so the law looms ever larger in popular consciousness. Christians unfortunately are not exempt from this idolatry.

Of all people we in the community of the faithful have the most reason to be on guard against false gods. The First Commandment is inexorable in what it requires of us, total fidelity to God, His Church, His Law. While what is Caesar's is shared by all Caesars, what is God's belongs to Him alone.

Idols have taken many different forms in human life. In Old Testament times they were more obvious. Recall the words of the Psalmist:[7]

> Their idols are silver and gold,
> the work of human hands.
> They have mouths; but they cannot speak;
> they have eyes; but they cannot see;

they have ears; but they cannot hear;
they have nostrils but they cannot smell.
With their hands they cannot feel;
with their feet they cannot walk.
No sound comes from their throats.
Their makers will come to be like them
and so will all who trust in them.

Today idols may be money, or sex, or beauty, or power, or social standing — or the law. And the law, because of its prestige, and because it may appear to some to go to the very heart of morality, may be the most insidious of all.

To my mind the question is not whether morality needs the support of the law, but rather whether we can afford to be lulled into a frame of mind in which we unthinkingly confuse our principles of Christian behaviour with the edicts of the law. It seems to me that our own Canadian Charter of Rights and Freedoms puts things in the right order. In its preamble it refers with solemn emphasis to the rule of law (by which we understand the primacy of law) but only after it has mentioned first the supremacy of God. The actual text is as follows:

> Whereas Canada is founded upon principles that recog-
> nize the supremacy of God and the rule of law ...

The Canadian bishops have, of course, a very sophisticated understanding of the relationship of law and morals. They go no further than to say:[8]

> The state has a key role to play in the formation of a col-
> lective conscience within the framework of a climate of social
> peace and respect for people who hold differing views.
> Recent legislation on smoking and drinking are good exam-
> ples of how the law shapes as well as reflects consensus.

This is true, primarily in the generically indifferent area of human acts, but it is accurate only insofar as there are no strong countervailing forces. The Church does not vacate the field, as has been emphasized in this chapter, where other moral issues are at stake, but either reinforces or counters the ped-agogical effect of the law, as the case may be. In this respect abortion is no exception.

Unlike Shakespeare's Antony, I have not come either to praise or to bury Caesar. The law has its own sphere, one to which I have in fact devoted the greater part of my life. Its work is a great one, a life-absorbing one. But it cannot substitute for the far higher role of the Church and its moral code. As long as the law stays within its democratic bounds, it cannot impede or thwart the moral imperative. If we keep it within its traditional limits and accept for the sake of democracy the views of the vast majority as to the law, we cannot be the losers. For we shall be acting in accord with the spirit of our democratic system, the most Christian-compatible form of government that has yet been devised. It was, after all, our Lord Himself who said "Render to Caesar the things that are Caesar's."

The present time, for Christians living in democracies, essentially characterized as they are by majority rule, is a time of testing, rather than of triumph. But I believe that, with an acceptance of the differences between law and morality, we can at least realize the negative achievement that in no other way can we do better, and that to do otherwise would be to do worse. In fact, we should have done all we can, consistent with the kind of democratic society that we rightly cherish. Our best choice is to leave the rest to Divine Providence.

In other words, the imperfect is the best of which the City of Man is capable. For perfection we must await the fullness of the City of God.

CHAPTER 12

FREEDOM AND RESPONSIBILITY FOR CHRISTIANS IN DEMOCRACY

Although it was sometimes said in the past that democracy is merely Christianity in secular dress, it is often thought to be more fashionable nowadays to assume that the political phenomenon of democracy is best served by a relativist morals. This is a view from which I sharply dissent.

No doubt there are Christians who do accept that morality is entirely relativist in terms of historical eras or different societies or just the unique circumstances of individual acts. Indeed, the Christian theological movement of "situation ethics" tends very much in this direction.

I would not want to diminish the very large societal and historical elements in morals. I believe in a minimalist rather than a maximalist natural law, with sociological and other elements playing a large role in the translation of the limited common basis into a more precisely fashioned ethic. To my mind the process is akin to that of the development of theological doctrine, to which I referred at the end of chapter 6.

My principal objection to tying democracy in with moral relativism is not that it allows for some indeterminacy in moral theory but that it limits democracy to a particular moral ideology. Democracy does, of course, involve substance or content as well as procedure, but its substantive content is very slender.

Professor John Hart Ely has recently argued that under the American Constitution judicial review "can appropriately concern itself only with the question of [political] participation, and not with the substantive merits of the political choice under attack,"[1] a theory he calls a "participation-oriented, representation-reinforcing approach to judicial review."[2] Whether or not he is correct in his analysis of American due process, the substantive connotation of democracy may not go much beyond the flowering of human rights, which may be thought of as the principal constituent of the common good.

This is particularly the case with the attainment of equality. As I put it some years ago:[3]

> Democracy implies not only equality in the selection of a government, or in the determination of policies (as in a referendum democracy), but also the pursuit of equality, especially equality of opportunity, as an economic, social, cultural and moral goal. It is because all men are fundamentally equal in their humanity that democracy is the most fully human form of government. It is because they are unequal in their natural endowments and social circumstances that democracy has to be achieved as well as posited, and that democracy as procedure is not a final end, but subordinated to the attainment of a more ultimate end, democracy as substance, viz,. genuine equality.

The French Revolutionary triad of "liberty, equality, fraternity" was not inaccurate as a summation of democracy. If the initial phenomenon of liberty is directed towards equality as its end, fraternity is a good description of the result.

❧❀❧

Democracy does not do the hard things well, because people as a whole are selfishly reluctant to vote to give up anything. William Pfaff has recently written of "a fundamental inability of governments responsive to popular opinion to deal with problems whose consequences lie in the future." He stated:[4]

> There are certain complacencies by which the democracies justify their aversion to sacrifice. We say that because the democracies are virtuous they will always win out in the end; the cold war has proved it. We say that awkward as the system may seem it is still better than all the rest. We say that democracies never fight other democracies, and the world is getting more democratic. We say the people always know best.
>
> The fact is that democracies compete badly with despotism. Democracies don't like sacrifices, or the politicians who demand them. Democracies are not good at looking after their security interests when a gun is not pointed at their heads. Democracies don't like to listen to bad news.

Democracies don't want to think about bad possibilities in the future. Democracies don't want their comfort or profits interfered with. Democracies may not win out in the long term. It is entirely possible that until now they have merely been lucky.

This is a bleak picture, but in my opinion is true in tendency, as most democratic politicians will testify. Overcoming the tendency requires exceptional leadership, particularly in a country like the United States with a constitutionally built-in bias against government.[5]

Democracy could well use large numbers of disinterested people, dedicated to the common good, to help it to rise to higher levels of awareness, achievement and, if need be, sacrifice. Christians could be such people.

Christianity has often been described as an other-worldly religion, and Catholics in particular have often gratefully accepted the accusation as a compliment on their perception of the higher values of life. "Work," I once wrote ironically, was looked on by Catholics as "a mandate of the Protestant ethic, thrift a prerogative of the Presbyterians, and capitalism an invention of the Calvinists. Worldly success, we rationalized, was not for Catholics, but for Protestants, Jews and agnostics."[6] Such a mentality does not, however, square with the attitude of *aggiornamento* contained in Vatican II's *Pastoral Constitution on The Church in the Modern World*:[7]

> They are mistaken who, knowing that we have here no abiding city but seek one which is to come, think that they may therefore shirk their earthly responsibilities ... The Christian who neglects his temporal duties neglects his duties towards his neighbour and even God, and jeopardizes his eternal salvation.

The faith itself requires that Christians measure up to their earthly responsibilities, but not all Christians share secular responsibilities to the same degree. It is the laity who "must take on the renewal of the temporal order as their own special obligation."[8] They are the Church's specialists in the secular city, precisely because they are themselves secular. To quote the *Dogmatic Constitution on the Church*:[9]

> A secular quality is proper and special to laymen ... [T]he laity, by their very vocation seek the kingdom of God by engaging in temporal affairs and by ordering them according to the plan of God.

The laity's very vocation is to order temporal affairs "according to the plan of God."

A Christian theologian who has cogently developed the theme of the Christian in the world is Dr. Harvey Cox in *The Secular City*, who lauds secularization as opposed to secularism.[10] Secularization is a social and cultural movement by which societies have been emerging from ecclesiastical control. It is marked by disestablishment through the separation of church and state and by pluralism and tolerance. It is for Cox an authentic consequence of Bible and faith. Secularism, on the other hand, is a new closed ideology which would deny the existence of any world but this, and which is thus intellectually hostile to religion. Secularization is for him as liberating as secularism is enslaving.

In Catholic terms, the theological foundation for the consequence of lay secularity is laid in the *Pastoral Constitution*, where it is asserted that the laity "are in their own way made sharers in the priestly, prophetic, and kingly functions of Christ."[11] The relevant function here is the kingly role, for the laity have dominion over the secular city, and it is theirs to decide how best to deal with its problems. Obviously, as history progresses, there will be a great deal more social and theological development in this area.

There is no doubt in my mind that this new theology tremendously extends the range of Catholics' freedom. They can now perceive their freedom to make choices in the whole secular area without any direction from the institutional Church except at the level of principle — this was, of course, a freedom which Christians always possessed but which a majority, perhaps, did not realize they had. In practical terms, they are almost completely on their own.[12]

This freedom also carries an onerous responsibility, and the laity will be judged by Almighty God on the conscientiousness with which they have exercised their freedom, because they alone are the Church in this department of life. If they fail, their part of the secular city fails with them, fails to gain the divine life which is its due. The responsibility is awesome indeed, but the freedom is magnificent. At last, humans are free beings like God — under God, of course, but also *like* God in being their own masters.[13]

A direct consequence of what I have called lay secularity is the necessity for collaboration with our neighbours, no matter how secularistic, or hedonistic or agnostic they may be, in the construction of the secular city. The *Decree on the Apostolate of the Laity* recognized the importance of such collaboration: "As citizens they [the laity] must co-operate with other citizens, using their particular skills and acting on their own responsibility."[14] So did the *Pastoral Constitution*, which stated that the laity "will gladly work with men seeking the same goals."[15] This is in keeping with the view of Pope John XXIII in his encyclical letter *Pacem in Terris* that believers should not refuse to work with Communists and other non-believers for the attainment of practical ends.[16]

A large barrier to cooperation in the past was caused by the failure of Christians to allow the state its own proper autonomy vis-à-vis the church. I have referred in chapter 4 to the recognition by the Canadian Catholic bishops that "the Christian legislator must make his own decisions" and that "religious and moral values ... enter into political decisions only insofar as they affect the common good." This principle of the common good so clearly represents not only the Christian tradition but also the best thinking of the present that it will surely come to be accepted by even the most recalcitrant hierarchies.

Democracies, like national hierarchies, are far from identical. In an analysis some years ago of democracies in terms of their basic values, Seymour Martin Lipset[17] found considerable differences even among the four large English-speaking democracies, viz., Australia, Canada, the United Kingdom and the United States, and drew the empirical generalization that Australia and the United States are more like each other than either is to Britain or to Canada. Canada is obviously much more like the United States than it is like Britain, but there are still marked differences.

The differences are particularly obvious constitutionally. The British Constitution, from which all of the others derive, is for the most part unwritten and is essentially evolutionary in its origin. The U.S. Constitution, on the other hand, expresses what I might call the "big bang" theory of constitutional creation, underscored by the gunfire of the American Revolution and "the rockets' red glare, the bombs bursting in air" of the U.S. national anthem. The revolutionary big bang occurred not only in sovereignty but also in constitutional conceptualization, and led to both the American separation of powers among the three branches of government and the U.S. constitutional entrenchment of individual rights, enforced through the review of the judiciary, the so-called "least dangerous branch."

The British parliamentary tradition was not marked by any such fear of governmental power but rather by a trust that parliamentary élites would act reasonably, for the common good of all and with a sense of responsibility towards minorities.

Canada as a country is set in the middle between the Unites States and the United Kingdom — geographically, institutionally, sociologically. With the United States, Canada shares federalism, and since 1982 a fundamental document protecting human rights. With the United Kingdom, it shares responsible government, and the tradition and concept of benign government. The most telling phrase in the powers of the Canadian parliament, as set forth in section 91 of the Constitution Act, 1867, is the overarching jurisdiction "to make Laws for the Peace, Order, and good Government of Canada." That is a world apart form the archetypal American "life, liberty and the pursuit of happiness" of the Declaration of Independence.

Yet, despite their differences, all of these — as well as other — democracies are distinguished by their possession of an open society. As I previously had occasion to describe it:[18]

> The open society is a synonym for democracy. Democracy has direct reference to the form of government based on universal franchise, but includes in its ambit of meaning many other social attributes which are either conceptually or actually necessary for its full realization. The open society, on the other hand, denotes the spirit of rational, critical and personal enquiry that animates democracy, enabling the individual person to make his own judgements, find his own values, and set his own life style. A person in an open society will function, not by reason of authority, but by the authority of reason. Socially, the open society refers to the fundamental freedoms which we normally guarantee in bills of rights, the freedoms which enable us to hold, to enjoy, and to proselytize personal and social values. It connotes, too, the openness of government and its operations to public scrutiny and to public influence, the openness of the political process in parties and their financing, the openness of social and economic structures (which we call social mobility), the openness of the majority to minority viewpoints and of minorities to the rights of the majority, and the openness of the whole of a national society to the rest of the world. In short, an open society means an open government, an open people, an open economic and social system, and ultimately an open world.

It is this concept of the open society which most fully specifies the content of the democratic social compact to which I have many times referred. It includes the commitment to fundamental freedoms, and particularly of course to the freedom of conscience. It also incorporates what I have called "the openness of the majority to minority viewpoints and of minorities to the rights of the majority."

Twenty-five years ago I believe I was right in writing that "both historically and contemporaneously the chief political issue dividing Catholics and Protestants [in Ontario] has been the school question."[19] But, as a result of intervening legislative and judicial developments, that is no longer the case.[20] What time has now made the principal bone of contention between Catholics and many others, not only in Ontario, but generally in Western democracies, is the abortion question. That is now the sticking point before all others.

I have already emphasized my conviction that both the theory and practice of democracy, grounded as they are in respect for freedom of conscience above all else, do not allow those who believe that abortion is morally wrong to use the criminal law to try to outlaw it. Such legislation would violate the first principle of democracy, it would not respect the democratic compact, and it would be incapable of enforcement.

In chapter 6 I referred to Jacques Maritain's conception of a progressive distinction in history between civil society and the spiritual realm of the Church, a separating out and clarifying of the things that are Caesar's from those that are God's. This process of desacralization of society is similar to the concept of secularization found in Harvey Cox. Inasmuch as it is possible to trace and understand the evolution of divine providence for the world, this development would seem to be an integral part of it, the best witness being that of Vatican II. The state is now seen to have its own role, democracy to be its most compatible form, the neutral state not professing the Catholic religion an advance, and the role of the laity in secular society a responsible one. The Vatican Council approved, after the fact, developments which had already taken place in society and in the Church, for actions often cannot await theology.[21] In the continued development of the scriptural distinction of the things of Caesar's, we are already on the way to new stages, compelled to a solution by the crisis of abortion, as the Church was led to an earlier stage of development by the then unwelcome loss of its power base in the Papal States. If Acton's insight is right, what is at the bottom of all this development is the continually expanding recognition of human conscience, which may be taken as metonymy for the human person as such.

The laity's vocation to order temporal affairs according to the plan of God is one that obviously has to be carried out without any direct knowledge of divine providence. The best we can do is to enter into new situations according to their own apparent dimensions, striving to see them as *they* are and to bring into them what *we* are.

Christians in democratic society therefore will be following the plan of God if they deal with it according to its own form and ethos. Christians cannot change the ground rules of democracy. But they can and should enliven it, enlighten it, and transform it, provided they can do so *from within.*

In matters where they cannot agree with the moral code of others living in the society, they should act as living witnesses to the truth as they know it, not adopting the lower morality embodied in the law, but displaying by their lives the higher morality in which they believe.

Christians therefore aim at revolutionizing society, not through the compulsion of law on the behaviour of others, but by changing the moral views of others so that they will not want to live by the bare minimum of the law but by the supererogation of a higher moral law. As John Paul II put it in *Veritatis Splendor,* "evangelization is the most powerful and stirring challenge which the Church has been called to face from her very beginning,"[22] and this new evangelization "also involves the proclamation and presentation of morality."[23]

The Christian challenge to society must be made, not through law, but through faith, hope and, above all, love.

NOTES

INTRODUCTION

1 This popular assumption, is, I believe, a common Catholic opinion. However, the serious orthodox case for the prohibition of abortion is based, like my own conclusion to the contrary, on an analysis of the common good, but one which does not give the same weight to the freedom of conscience. The orthodox case is presented in chapter 4.

2 Report of the Committee on Homosexual Offences and Prostitution, Cmnd. 247, Her Majesty's Stationery Office, 1957, 24, par. 61. I discuss the views of the Canadian Catholic bishops in relation to the Wolfenden Report in chapter 4.

3 Daniel Callahan, *Abortion: Law, Choice and Morality*, The Macmillan Company, 1970, 438. Callahan now describes himself as a "cultural — as distinguished from an active — practicing Catholic": "The Abortion Debate: Is Progress Possible?" in *Abortion: Understanding Differences*, ed. Sidney and Daniel Callahan, Plenum Press, 1984, 309. Of course, he wrote what I quote during his more Catholic period.

4 This is also the case with Catholic judges, as witness American Justices William J. Brennan, Jr., and Anthony M. Kennedy (Antonin Scalia is to the contrary), as well as Canadian judges too numerous to name.

5 I am not alone among Catholic commentators in taking such a position. Daniel Callahan, *supra* note 3, 493, wrote in 1970:

"The only limitations [to human freedom in pluralistic societies] are upon those actions which seem to present clear and present dangers to the common good, and even there the range of prohibited actions is diminishing as more and more choices are left to personal and private decisions. I have contended that, apart from some regulating laws, abortion decisions should be left, finally, up to the women themselves. Whatever one may think of the morality of abortion, it cannot be established that it poses a clear and present danger to the common good."

Fr. Patrick Hannan, Professor of Moral Theology, St. Patrick's College, Maynooth, Ireland, *Church, State, Morality and Law*, Christian Classics, Inc., 1992, 124, stated more recently that:

"[I]t is difficult to fault the response of Governor Cuomo and other U.S. politicians who are Catholic and yet claim the freedom to make up their own minds upon the question of abortion legislation and the concomitant issue of the provision of public funding for abortion."

Norman St. John Stevas sought rather to prevent abortion-on-demand by supporting a moderate measure of abortion law reform: "The English Experience," *America*, 9 Dec. 1967, 707. Where I may be different from earlier commentators is in basing my position principally upon the freedom of conscience.

6 Governor Cuomo's address was delivered to the Notre Dame Department of Theology on 13 September 1984. It was entitled "Religious Belief and Public Morality: A Catholic Governor's Perspective." I quote from

pages 4 and 13. The address was substantially excepted by the New York *Times*, 14 Sept. 1984, A21.

7 Éditions Paulines, 1993, n. 60 at 92. Another indication of the sacredness of conscience is Canon 748(2) which provides that "It is never lawful for anyone to force others to embrace the Catholic faith against their conscience": The *Code of Canon Law in English Translation*, Collins, Canadian Conference of Catholic Bishops, 1983. Church documents always link conscience with truth. Thus Canon 748(1) provides that "All are bound to seek the truth in the matters which concern God and his Church: when they have found it, then by divine law they are bound, and they have the right, to embrace and keep it." The Canadian Catholic bishops issued a helpful "Statement on the Formation of Conscience" in 1973, reprinted in *Love Kindness! The Social Teaching of the Canadian Catholic Bishops (1958–1989): A Second Collection*, ed. E.F. Sheridan, S.J., Éditions Paulines and the Jesuit Centre for Social Faith and Justice, 1991, 159–175.

8 *Supra* note 7, n. 31 at 52. It should, of course, be said that the Pontiff does not draw the same conclusions I do with respect to abortion from the imperative character of conscience.

9 University of Chicago Press, 1951, 110, 117, 118, respectively.

10 410 U.S. 113 (1973). The quotation is found at 165. The inner dynamics of this case have recently been spelled out in David J. Garrow, *Liberty and Sexuality: The Right to Privacy and the Making of Roe* v. *Wade*, Macmillan, 1984.

11 *Planned Parenthood of Southeastern Pennsylvania* v. *Casey*, 112 S. Ct. 2791, 2811 (1992). These judges, while admitting that "advances in neonatal care have advanced viability to a point somewhat earlier" (*ibid.*), point out that this affects only the timing and not the principle.

12 *Life's Dominion: An Argument about Abortion, Euthanasia and Individual Freedom*, Alfred A. Knopf, 1993, 160ff.

13 *R.* v. *Morgentaler (No. 2)*, [1988] 1 S.C.R. 30.

14 *Supra* note 7, n. 115 at 172. Despite its profound and prayerful passages, Bernhard Häring, *"Veritatis Splendor* in Focus: 2 — A Distrust That Wounds," *The Tablet*, 23 Oct. 1993, 1378, writes:

> *"Veritatis Splendor* contains many beautiful things. But almost all real splendour is lost when it becomes evident that the whole document is directed above all towards one goal: to endorse total assent and submission to all utterances of the Pope, and above all on one crucial point: that the use of any artificial means for regulating birth is intrinsically evil and sinful, without exception even in circumstances where contraception would be a lesser evil."

Professor Nicholas Lash, *Veritatis Splendor* in Focus: 5 — "Teaching in Crisis," *The Tablet*, 13 Nov. 1993, 1480, 1481, sees the encyclical in the same way and refers to "what is perhaps the most embarrassing sentence in the encyclical." He quotes and comments:

> "'With regard to intrinsically evil acts, and in reference to contraceptive practices ... Pope Paul VI teaches' (80; there follows a quotation from *Humanae Vitae*). This sentence is embarrassing because Pope Paul VI did not say that contraception was intrinsically evil (*malum*) but intrinsically 'inhonestum.' And the one thing clear about the meaning of this word is that it was chosen in order to *avoid* saying 'malum.'"

In a subsequent letter, *The Tablet*, 18 Dec. 1993, 1655, Msgr. Basil Loftus points out that the Latin term *"inhonestum* is capable of and indeed favours, a translation which does not even amount to 'bad.'" The controversy continued with a rebuttal by Professor John Finnis in a letter in the issue of 5 February 1994, and a further reply by Professor Lash in that of 12 February 1994.

Another problem with the encyclical is its attack on theological "straw men" and its failure to come to grips with the actual complexities of "current" theology: Richard McCormick, S.J., *"Veritatis Splendor* in Focus: Killing the Patient," *The Tablet*, 30 Oct. 1993, 1410, writes to that effect with respect to "proportionalism," and Joseph Fuchs, S.J., " *Veritatis Splendor in Focus: 4* — Good Acts and Good Persons," *The Tablet*, 6 Nov. 1993, 1444, regarding the theory of the "fundamental option."

15 *Supra* note 7, n. 97 at 146–7.

16 My 1966 address to the Michaelmas Conference in Toronto was published the following year: "The Christian and Politics," (1967) 10 *The Basilian Teacher* 204.

17 The Hon. Mr. Turner used those words in the House of Commons: *Debates*, 23 January 1969, 4722.

18 *Supra* note 13.

19 F.L. Morton, *Morgentaler v. Borowski: Abortion, the Charter, and the Courts*, McClelland & Stewart, Inc., 1992, 313.

20 Robert F. Drinan, S.J., "The Right of the Foetus to Be Born" (1967–8), 514 *Dublin Review* 365, appeared to endorse the arguments he advanced for a no-law solution during the first 26 weeks of pregnancy. Such a system would have "the undeniable virtue of neutralizing the law so that, while the law does not forbid abortion, it does not on the other hand sanction it" (371). The reference to 26 weeks is at 381. Drinan gives three reasons for the value of a non-law: (1) the impossibility of enforcement of a law limiting abortion; (2) the interference with family life in requiring the birth of an unwanted child; (3) the escalation of illegal abortions (which historical experience shows accompanies partial legalization) leads people to think that any reason really suffices.

21 The Attorney General's view is commented upon in an editorial in the *Canadian Register*, 28 Apr. 1967.

22 House of Commons *Debates*, 24 January 1969, 4793–4. I also spoke in the debate on 6 May 1969, 8396, during the report stage to support a private member's "two-adverbs amendment," which would have added the adverbs "seriously" and "directly" to qualify the degree of danger to a mother's life or health which would permit therapeutic abortion. I had made the same amendment myself in the Standing Committee on Justice and Legal Affairs. It lost on both occasions.

23 The trial decision in this case, which took place during my time as Minister, is reported as *Borowski* v. *Canada,* [1984] 1 W.W.R. 15. The story of this trial told in F.L. Morton, *supra* note 19, 131–53.

24 In *Reference re B.C. Motor Vehicle Act*, [1985] 2 S.C.R. 486, 504–5, Lamer J. (as he then was) quoted the view expressed in parliamentary committee for the government by Assistant Deputy Minister B.L. Strayer (as he then was) as to the intended meaning of the phrase "the fundamental principles of law" in s. 7 of the Charter only to dismiss it as unduly limiting. The government spokesman had said:

> "Mr. Chairman, it was our belief that the words "fundamental justice" would cover the same thing as what is called procedural due process, that is the meaning of due process in relation to requiring fair procedure. However, it in our view does not cover the

concept of what is called substantive due process, which
would impose substantive
requirements as to policy of
the law in question.

This has been most clearly
demonstrated in the United
States in the area of property,
but also in other areas such as
the right to life. The term due
process has been given the
broader concept of meaning
both the procedure and substance. Natural justice or fundamental justice in our view
does not go beyond the procedural requirements of fairness."

As one present at the first meeting of
then Justice Minister Trudeau's advis-
ers on the incipient Charter in 1967, I
can confirm from personal experience
that s. 7 was intended from the first
moment of conceptualization to be
limited to the procedural requirements
of fairness, and that that was the general understanding when the Charter
became part of the Canadian
Constitution in 1982. At least from the
B.C. Motor Vehicle Reference in 1985
on, however, it was clear that it would
not be so interpreted by the Supreme
Court of Canada.

25 L.W. Sumner, *Abortion and Moral
Theory*, Princeton University Press,
1981, 29, 40, 82, respectively.
Nevertheless, F.M. Kamm, *Creation
and Abortion: A Study in Moral and
Legal Philosophy*, Oxford University
Press, 1992, questions whether abortion would not be permissible even if a
fetus were acknowledged to have the
rights of a person.

26 Muldoon J. put it as follows in
*O'Sullivan v. Minister of National
Revenue*, [1992] 1 F.C. 522, 542:

[W]hile the secular State is
bound to defend, that is to
guarantee everyone's freedom
of conscience and religion, it
is not bound or even permitted, to promote every expres-

sion or manifestation of conscience and religion, just as it
is not bound to promote every
manifestation of freedom of
opinion and expression, some
of which are defamatory.

In the light of my thesis, one might
perhaps query the Court's holding that
the legal compulsion to pay taxes to
fund abortion services, a use which
offended the taxpayer's religious
beliefs, is justified only under s. 1 of
the Charter and not under s. 2 (*a*).

27 Of course, the first three members of
"freedom of thought, belief, opinion
and expression, including freedom of
the press and other media of communi-
cation" in s. 2 (*b*) of the Canadian
Charter could also be considered internal and absolute freedoms, if not read
as governed by the freedom of expression. To the extent that they are interi-
or and are principles of ethical conduct, I would assimilate them to freedom of conscience.

28 "Abortion, Sex and Gender: The
Church's Public Voice," *America*, 22
May 1993, 6, 9. At the time of the
address Professor Cahill was president
of the Catholic Theological Society of
America.

29 Laurence H. Tribe, *Abortion: The
Clash of Absolutes*, W.W. Norton &
Company, New Paperback ed., 1992,
230.

30 *Ibid.*, 222. Professor Tribe also comments, 227:

The prospect of artificial
wombs ... raises justified fears
about a Brave New World of
state-run baby farms, including the spectre of state control
over the disposition of fetuses
that are not wanted by their
biological parents but that
develop under state command
into viable infants, some of
them perhaps badly handi-
capped.

31 "Human Life is Sacred," Pastoral
Letter of the Irish Bishops, May 1975,

reprinted in *Euthanasia: Recent Declarations of Popes and Bishops*, Life Ethics Centre, 1983, nn. 49 and 52, at 12–13.

32 "Ireland: Abortion Returns to the Hustings," Note, *The Tablet*, 17 Oct. 1992, 1308.

CHAPTER 1

1 Bernhard Häring, "The Encyclical Crisis," *Commonweal*, 6 Sept. 1968, 588, writes that "no papal teaching has ever caused such an earthquake in the Church as the encyclical *Humanae Vitae.*" I realize that *Humanae Vitae* has twentieth-century competition for this dubious distinction, particularly from the encyclicals *Pascendi* (Pius X) in 1907 and *Humani Generis* (Pius XII) in 1950. *Pascendi dominici gregis*, to give it its fuller name, along with *Lamentabile sane exitu* (a Holy Office decree issued two months earlier) and the oath against modernism prescribed in September 1910, constituted the Church's reaction to modernism, which may be loosely described as the intellectual effect on the Church of nineteenth-century evolution — biological, historical and theological. *Humani Generis* dealt with Divine Revelation, particularly Sacred Scripture. Both of these encyclicals caused years of anguish for theologians because of their sweeping nature of their condemnations, but for the most part they did not directly affect the whole Church, and I therefore judge them to have been less calamitous than *Humanae Vitae*, which so directly touches the laity.

When I speak of *Humanae Vitae* and its deficiencies in this chapter, I am referring only to its most notable teaching, that on contraception. On the other hand, the five characteristics of conjugal love set out in the encyclical (human, total, faithful and exclusive, fruitful and moral) have become ground-breaking principles for the work of Catholic marriage tribunals.

2 One small measure of the encyclical's lack of persuasion is that immediately after the publication of the Encyclical more that 650 American Catholic theologians issued a statement of dissent. Of course, there are also theologians who support *Humanae Vitae*. One of the books most strongly in favour of its position, although written beforehand, is Germain Grisez's *Contraception and the Natural Law*, Bruce, 1964.

3 Sebastian Moore, O.S.B., "Crisis over Contraception," *The Tablet*, 7 October 1989, at 1148, comments: "The tendency now is always to mention contraception and abortion together, so that contraception may seem to participate in the clear evil of abortion. It has been observed that the Pope [John Paul II] hardly ever mentions the one without the other." There were suggestions, shortly after the publication of *Humanae Vitae*, that Pope Paul VI was trying to soften its impact. The Ottawa *Journal*, 18 July 1970, 45, reports, for instance, a papal statement implying that the use of contraceptives is not necessarily the kind of sin that makes a Catholic unworthy to receive the sacraments. Pope John Paul II has followed a much harder line and seems to have made opposition to contraception a test of orthodoxy. Of course, it remains true that abortion is matter for excommunication whereas contraception is not. *The Code of Canon Law in English Translation*, Collins, Canadian Conference of Catholic Bishops 1983, can. 1398 states that "a person who actually procures an abortion incurs a *latae sententiae* excommunication" [i.e., one which is incurred automatically upon the commission of the offence, without having to be specifically imposed]. No special sanction is provided for contraception.

4 E.E.Y. Hales, *Pio Nono: A Study in European Politics and Religion in the 19th Century*, Eyre & Spottiswoode, 2nd ed., 1956, points out that, although the *Syllabus* was not signed by the Pope, it was sent out with his encycli-

cal *Quanta Cura* and under his authority. Its full title shows it to be a compendium of other writings by the Pontiff: "A Syllabus, containing the principal Errors of our times, which are noted in the Consistorial Allocations, in the Encyclicals, and in other apostolic letters of our most Holy Lord, Pope Pius IX." Although the original project of a syllabus was set on foot in 1852, the final commission that produced the *Syllabus* did its work after the loss of most of the papal states and in the atmosphere of that time, and the 76th of the condemned theses was that "the abrogation of the civil power that the Holy See has acquired would be conducive to the liberty and well-being of the Church."

The last of the eighty propositions adjudged by the Pope to be erroneous was as follows: "The Roman Pontiff can and should reconcile and harmonize himself with progress, with liberalism, and with recent civilization." The 77th erroneous proposition was that "in our age it is no longer expedient that the Catholic Religion should be regarded as the sole religion of the State to the exclusion of all others." In the words of the historian Roger Aubert, *Le Pontificat de Pie Neuf*, 1952, 255, "the majority of Catholics were stupefied by the *Syllabus*."

5 *Veritatis Splendor* ("The Splendor of Truth"), Éditions Paulines, 1993, n. 80, at 123–4.

6 As it was put, *ibid.*, n. 64 at 97, "Christians have a great help for the formation of conscience in *the Church and her Magisterium.*" Nicholas Lash, "Veritatis Splendor in Focus: 5 — Teaching in Crisis," *The Tablet*, 13 Nov. 1993, 1480, points out that this encyclical restricts the *magisterium* to the Pope and his advisors, whereas it had originally extended to the episcopate as a whole.

7 "A Coup for the Pope," *The Tablet*, 2 Oct. 1993, 1251; "Rome Prepares to Launch Encyclical," *The Tablet*, 2 Oct. 1993, 1270.

8 See, e.g., Peter Hebblethwaite, "The Limits of Infallibility," *The Tablet*, 14 Aug. 1993, 1036, who argues that *Humanae Vitae* is not and cannot be infallible. However, Germain Grisez, *"Veritatis Splendor* in Focus: 1 — Revelation versus Dissent," *The Tablet*, 16 Oct. 1993, 1329, maintains that "in claiming that the received teaching concerning intrinsically evil acts is a revealed truth, the Pope also implicitly asserts that it is definable," and Grisez calls for the *magisterium* infallibly to define it.

Fr. Seán Fagan S.M. takes Grisez to task for his fundamentalist views in a letter, *The Tablet*, 20 Nov. 1993 1519:

> "Grisez insists that "the teaching concerning intrinsically evil acts is a revealed truth," but is faith not unreasonably tested when paragraph 14 of *Humanae Vitae* absolutely forbids contraceptive pills, but in the following paragraph allows them "for therapy" — the same pills, working in accordance with God's same laws of physiology and producing the same effect? If Grisez's assertion is true, Catholics will be amazed at the "revealed truths" they are bound to believe because they are found in encyclicals or council declarations. The Council of Florence declared that all heathens, Jews, heretics and schismatics go to hell unless converted to the Catholic Church. Pope Leo declared that the burning of heretics is in accord with the will of the Holy Spirit. Four ecumenical councils sanctioned slavery as a lawful practice for Christians.
>
> "During the thirteenth century six different popes justified and authorised the use of torture. Freedom of conscience was condemned by Pius IX as

sheer madness. The 1931 encyclical of Pius XI on Christian education solemnly declared that "coeducation (male and female together) is erroneous and pernicious, and often based on a naturalism which denies original sin ... Nature itself, which makes the two sexes different in organism, inclinations and attitudes, provides no argument for mixing them promiscuously, much less educating them together." The papal condemnation of co-education and artificial means of family planning both appeal to "nature" as the basis for their argument. What kind of "nature" are they talking about? Does "nature" still declare that marriage is primarily for procreation?

"Professor Grisez may find some way to explain away these "teachings of the Church," held and imposed in some cases for centuries, but the God-given common sense of Christians will see it as a whitewash, and if they are upset to find themselves at odds with some official teaching of encyclicals they can be consoled when they realised how radically the Church has changed its teaching through the years, though it still makes no apology for the appalling suffering it caused to legal dissenters who saw more clearly than their teachers. The Church's credibility as a teaching authority is greatly lessened when it has fundamentalist defenders like Professor Grisez ..."

9 John T. Noonan, Jr., *Contraception: A History of Its Treatment by the Catholic Theologians and Canonists*, enlarged ed., The Bellnap Press of Harvard University Press, 1986 at 532.

10 *Five Great Encyclicals*, ed. Gerald C. Treacy, S.J., The Paulist Press, 1939, nn. 54–5, at 92.

11 Noonan, *supra* note 9 at 35, writes: "Was Onan punished for his disobedience, for his lack of family feeling, for his egotism, for his evasion of an obligation assumed, for his contraceptive acts, or for a combination of these faults? ... That contraception as such is condemned seems unlikely. There is no commandment against contraception in any of the codes of law." St. Jerome's unsatisfactory translation of the Book of Genesis for the Latin Vulgate edition added to the likelihood of misinterpretation: *ibid.* at 101–2.

12 (1951) 43 *Acta Apostolicae Sedis*, 845–6. The English translation is that quoted by Jack Dominian, " '*Humanae Vitae*' Revisited (2): The Flaw in the Tradition," *The Tablet*, 3 Nov. 1984, 1083, 1084.

13 At the end, the theologians and the bishops on the Commission voted separately (15 to 4 against the ban in the case of the theologians, and 9 to 3 with 3 abstentions in the case of the bishops, with the future John Paul II not participating): "Majority's position favoured by 9 to 3," *National Catholic Reporter*, 25 Sept. 1968, 1. Peter Hebblethwaite, *Paul VI: The First Modern Pope*, Paulist Press, 1993, 469, reports that "on June 28 [1966] the co-President of the Commission, Cardinal Julius Döpfner, and its secretary Henri de Riedmatten OP were able to present to Paul the final report which concluded that the Catholic position on artificial conception 'could not be sustained by reasoned argument.'" The whole of the Commission's Final Report is reprinted in Robert Kaiser, *Sex, Politics and Religion: A Case History in the Development of Doctrine, 1962–1984*, Leaven Press, 1985, 248–58. Other information is contained in Arthur McCormack, "Marriage and Birth Control," *The Tablet*, 31 May 1986, 556, 558.

14 "On the Encyclical *Humanae Vitae*," *National Catholic Reporter*, 18 September 1968, 6, a translation of an article which appeared in the September 1968 issue of *Stimmen der Zeit*.

15 Janet E. Smith, *Humanae Vitae: A Generation Later*, The Catholic University of America Press, 1991, Appendix One, 280–284. I refer to "the Curial authors" because of the internal testimony of Bernhard Häring, C.Ss.R.: "Curia controlled Pope's decision," *National Catholic Reporter*, 21 Aug. 1968, 6, where he writes, inter alia, "I have evidence, enough evidence for the formation of my own conscience — it was a test case for the curia to affirm that papal encyclicals stand higher than the council decrees."

16 Spoken in private conversation and quoted by Moore, *supra* note 3, 1146. Moore, 1147, refers to the papal biology in *Humanae Vitae* as "a kind of mystical biology, with a virtual equation of Mother Nature with God."

17 *Supra* note 14, 6. As Rahner points out, the only valid question is not whether human beings possess such a right but whether in a particular case the moral limits of such self-manipulation have been exceeded or not. Fr. Bernhard Häring, C.Ss.R., has laid great emphasis on the analogy between contraception and the use of drugs or surgery to preserve life or health: *The Tablet* reports on his approach, 4 Feb. 1989, 142, in relation to an article of his in the Italian review Il Regno.

18 "Rape, Abortion and Contraceptives," *Civiltà Cattolica*, 3 July 1993. E.E.Y. Hales, *The Catholic Church in the Modern World*, Image Books Ed. 1960, at 105–6 describes *Civiltà Cattolica* as "an authoritative (though not an official) vehicle of Catholic thought on religious and political matters."

19 If the teaching of the official Church were not to the effect that contraception is equally wrong outside marriage, we might expect to find the episcopacy supporting rather than opposing school campaigns for the use of condoms in extramarital sex, at least as a second line of defence.

20 "The *Humanae Vitae* Crisis (1): Inside The Commission," *The Tablet*, 24 July 1993, 938.

21 *Supra* note 10, n. 23 at 83.

22 *Ibid.*, n. 24 at 84.

23 *Ibid.*, n. 23 at 93–4.

24 *The Documents of Vatican II*, ed. Walter M. Abbott, S.J., Guild Press, 1966, at 250–3.

25 In my view this is the case even though they cite some Vatican II documents, since the approach is not compatible with that of the Council. Bernhard Häring, *supra* note 1, writes:

"In my opinion it is harder to reconcile *Humanae Vitae* with the Council Constitution on *The Church in the Modern World* than to reconcile the Declaration on Religious Freedom with the *Syllabus* of Pius IX, or at least no less difficult. This assertion is based especially on the fact (1) that the question just mentioned from the Council Constitution [n. 51] and the text of 1 Cor. 7 ["The husband must give the wife what is due to her, and the wife must give the husband his due"] are simply not taken seriously, (2) that the conception of natural law of the whole pastoral Constitution of the Council has simply not been incorporated into *Humanae Vitae*, and (3) that the criteria worked out in the Constitution for the acceptability of methods of birth control are not even mentioned and simply replaced by biological 'laws.'"

26 "Abortion, Sex and Gender: The Church's Public Voice," *America*, 22 May 1993, 6, 10.

27 *Ibid.*

28 Windsor *Star*, 28 Sept. 1968, A20. The
    Catholic Bishops of Austria also took
    the position that Austrian Catholics
    may practice birth control if their con-
    sciences permit: Windsor *Star*, 28 Feb.
    1969, 6. In its statement on the 25th
    anniversary of *Humanae Vitae* of 22
    September 1993 the Canadian
    Conference of Catholic Bishops avoid-
    ed the direct moral issues of the
    encyclical entirely and dwelt on natur-
    al family planning.

29 *Ibid.*

30 "A Letter to the Pope," *The Tablet*, 30
    June 1990, 841–2.

31 *Maclean's* Magazine, 12 April 1993.

32 The Toronto *Globe and Mail*, 24 July
    1993, A7. The subsequent poll in
    Newsweek, 16 August 1993, 40, shows
    that only 62 percent of American
    Catholics consider the Catholic
    Church's position too conservative.
    This lower-than-usual percentage may
    perhaps be accounted for by differ-
    ences in sampling or by the vagueness
    of the question.

33 In *On Consulting the Faithful in
    Matters of Doctrine*, ed. John Coulson,
    G. Chapman, 1961, Newman related
    how the Catholic people preserved the
    faith against Arianism after the
    Council of Nicaea. As principal wit-
    nesses to revelation, the faithful have
    the right to be consulted in matters of
    doctrine: see *Final Report, Anglican-
    Roman Catholic International
    Commission*, SPCK and the Catholic
    Truth Society, 1982, Authority in the
    Church II, par. 25 at 92.

34 "The *Humanae Vitae* Crisis (3):
    Consulting the Faithful," *The Tablet*
    24 July 1993, 941.

35 "Building a Creative Conscience," *The
    Commonweal*, 11 Aug. 1989, 433,
    434.

36 "'*Humanae Vitae*': What Has It Done
    to Us?," *The Commonweal*, 18 June
    1993, 12, 13.

37 "'*Humanae Vitae*' Revisited (3):
    Beyond Biology," *The Tablet*, 10 Nov.
    1984, 1118.

38 *Ibid.*, 1119.

39 Such a personalist approach was per-
    haps first developed by Dietrich von
    Hildebrand in *In Defence of Purity*,
    New York, 1931, and by Fr. Herbert
    Doms, *The Meaning of Marriage*,
    Sheed & Ward, 1939.

40 John M. Haas, "The Inseparability of
    the Two Meanings of the Marriage
    Act" in *Reproductive Technologies,
    Marriage and the Church*, The Pope
    John Center, 1968, 89–106, is quite
    right in referring to the inseparable
    connection between the unitive mean-
    ing and the procreative meaning of
    conjugal love. Where in my view he is
    mistaken is in maintaining that these
    must both be present in every conjugal
    act, since they are not, for instance, in
    acts performed during the monthly
    time of infertility or after conception.
    That is why the Council Fathers wrote
    that "Personal love and sexual plea-
    sure together form the essence of the
    sexual act, *not the biological
    potential.*" (emphasis added)

41 *Maclean's* poll, *supra* note 31.

42 *Newsweek* poll, *supra* note 32. The
    American Church now has more fun-
    damental matters of unbelief (such as
    in the "real presence") to be worried
    about: N.Y. *Times*, 1 June 1994, A1.

43 The phrase is that of Dr. Dominian,
    "'*Humanae Vitae*' Revisited (4): The
    Need for Reform," *The Tablet*, 17
    Nov. 1984, 1146, 1147.

CHAPTER 2

1 *Pastoral Constitution on the Church in
   the Modern World* in *The Documents
   of Vatican II*, ed. Walter M. Abbott,
   S.J., Guild Press, 1966, n. 51 at 256.

2 On the history of Catholic thought
   with respect to abortion see Daniel
   Callahan, *Abortion: Law, Choice and
   Morality*, The Macmillan Company,

1970; Albert C. Outler, "The Beginnings of Personhood: Theological Considerations" (1973), 27 *Perkins Journal* 28–34; John R. Connery, S.J., *Abortion: The Development of the Roman Catholic Perspective*, Loyola University Press, 1977.

3 This view of Canadian criminal law before 1969 is sometimes disputed. I explained my position at House of Commons *Debates*, 24 Jan. 1969, 4793–4.

4 See Laurence H. Tribe, *Abortion: The Clash of Absolutes*, W.W. Norton & Company, new paper ed., 1992, 27ff.

5 *Five Great Encyclicals*, ed. Gerald C. Treacy, S.J., The Paulist Press, 1939, n. 63 at 94.

6 *Ibid.*, n. 64 at 95.

7 *Supra* note 1, n. 51 at 255–6.

8 The genetic material, DNA, cannot be enough to determine humanness because identical twins have the same DNA in the same maternal environment but have different fingerprints and are obviously distinct beings. See also note 9, infra. It may also become significant that a university researcher has recently cloned human embryos, by splitting single embryos into identical twins or triplets: New York *Times*, 24 Oct. 1993, 22. Technically, the term "zygote" is used from conception to three weeks, "embryo" from four to seven weeks, and "fetus" from the end of the eighth week to birth.

9 Joseph Danceel, "Immediate Animation and Delayed Terminization" (1970), 31 *Theological Studies* 76; James Diamond, "Abortion, Animation and Delayed Terminization" (1975), 36 *Theological Studies* 305; Thomas A. Shannon and Allan B. Wolter, O.F.M. (1990), 51 *Theological Studies* 603; John Mahoney, S.J., *Bioethics and Belief*, Sheed and Ward, 1984; Richard A. McCormick, S.J., "Who or What is the Pre-embryo?" (1991), 1 *Kennedy*

Institute of Ethics Journal 1. Shannon and Wolter say squarely, at 608, that "to become a human embryo, further essential and supplementary genetic information to what can be found in the zygote itself is required." Further, at 625: "Given the findings of modern biology, there is no evidence for the presence of a separate ontological individual until the completion of either restriction or gastrulation, which occurs around three weeks after fertilization. Therefore there is no reasonable basis for arguing that the pre-embryo is morally equivalent to a person or is a person as a basis for prohibiting abortion."

10 Jean M. Mills, "The Embryo: Not a Thing but a Process" (1986), 12 *Journal of Medical Ethics* 32.

11 Stephen D. Schwarz, *The Moral Question of Abortion*, Loyola University Press, 1990, 3–4. This account is from a Friend of the Court brief filed before the U.S. Supreme Court by a group of more than two hundred physicians.

12 Ronald Dworkin, *Life's Dominion: An Argument about Abortion, Euthanasia and Individual Freedom*, Alfred A. Knopf, 1993, 32–3. Professor Dworkin holds leading professorships at both Oxford and New York Universities.

13 *How Brave a New World? Dilemmas in Bioethics*, Georgetown University Press, 1981, 178. See also Lise Sowle Cahill, "Abortion, Sex and Gender: The Church's Public voice," *America*, 22 May 1993, 6, 8, on the importance of nuance in this area: "Doubts about the personhood of the fetus are not always due to wilful ignorance or malice and defenders of early abortion are not necessarily committed to the right of women to kill babies."

14 Déclaration des évêques belges sur l'avortement (1973), 70 Documentation catholique 434.

15 *Supra* note 5, n. 66 at 95.

16 New York *Times*, 15 Sept. 1984, 29.

17 The spokesman for the fifty-five theologians, Professor Daniel C. Maguire of Marquette University, answered Archbishop O'Connor in a letter to the New York *Times*, 16 Sept. 1984, 22E, referring in particular to theological disagreement on the moment of animation.

18 *The Abortion Papers: Inside the Abortion Mentality*, Frederick Fell, 1983, 150. He also notes that in fetal surgery, the child in the uterus is treated as a patient in his/her own right.

19 *Supra* note 11, 14.

20 *Supra* note 11, 45.

21 Dworkin, *supra* note 12, 11, writes that "human life is sacred just in itself; and ... the sacred nature of a human life begins when its biological life begins, even before the creature whose life it is has movement or sensation or interests or rights of its own."

22 "Contemporary Protestant Thinking," *America*, 9 Dec. 1967, 713.

23 John T. Noonan, Jr., *A Private Choice: Abortion in America in the Seventies*, The Free Press, 1979, 61, takes the similar position that in the 1970's "the major Protestant churches continued to maintain the traditional Christian condemnation of the act" of abortion.

24 *Church Dogmatics*, III, 4, 415–6, quoted by Drinan, *supra* note 22 at 714.

25 *Supra* note 22, 714.

26 James M. Gustafson, "A Protestant Ethical Approach," in *The Morality of Abortion: Legal and Historical Perspectives*, ed. John T. Noonan, Jr., Harvard University Press, 1970, 101, 122.

27 "Abortion: An Ecumenical Dilemma," *Commonweal*, 30 Nov. 1973, 231.

28 *Ibid.*, 235.

29 L.W. Sumner, *Abortion and Moral Theory*, Princeton University Press, 1981, 50–1.

30 *Supra* note 4, 131–2.

31 *Supra* note 4, 239.

32 "Religious Belief and Public Morality: A Catholic Governor's Perspective," An Address at the University of Notre Dame, 13 Sept. 1984, 10. The address is substantially reproduced in the New York *Times*, 14 Sept. 1984, A21.

33 *Supra* note 12, 33.

34 *Supra* note 12, 33.

35 *Supra* note 12, 33.

36 "The Future of Abortion," *The Tablet*, 23 Mar. 1985, 302, 303.

37 This is the title of Professor Tribe's book, *supra* note 4.

CHAPTER 3

1 *New Testament*, James 1:22

2 *Ibid.*, 2:14–16.

3 [1917] A.C. 406, 464–5.

4 [1932] A.C. 562, 580.

5 Encyclical Letter *Centesimus Annus*, Éditions Paulines, 1991, n. 46 at 83.

6 See, e.g., F. Donald Logan, *Excommunication and the Secular Arm in Medieval England*, Pontifical Institute of Mediaeval Studies, 1968.

CHAPTER 4

1 The address at Fordham University was excerpted by the New York *Times*, 7 Dec. 1983, B8.

2 The whole of this statement is reproduced in the New York *Times*, 14 Oct. 1984, 30. This statement was made only a day or two after the National Coalition of American Nuns with some 2,000 members opposed the criminalization of abortion and accused the bishops of sexism: Ottawa *Citizen*, 11 Oct. 1984, A18.

3 The phrase is that of Daniel Callahan, *Abortion: Law, Choice and Morality*, The Macmillan Company, 1970, 437.

4 Hans Lotstra, *Abortion: The Catholic Debate in America*, Irvington Publishers, Inc., 1985, 286–7.

5 N.Y. *Times*, 15 June 1990, A1.

6 N.Y. *Times*, 25 June 1990, A1.

7 To the best of my knowledge the only Canadian public figure who has been episcopally harassed in Canada in recent years is Maureen McTeer, who was already a high-profile pro-choice figure when she was nominated as the Progressive Conservative candidate in Carleton-Gloucester, an Ottawa-area riding, in the federal election on 21 November 1988. The Friday before the Monday election, in a press release issued by Campaign Coalition Life, Auxiliary Bishop Gilles Belisle of the Ottawa Archdiocese stated that an article Ms. McTeer had written explaining her position on abortion was "an offence to the Church and a distortion of Catholic teaching." Under threat of an action for defamation and after a 30-minute telephone conversation with Ms. McTeer, on Friday afternoon the Bishop sent her a signed apology in which he said that he regretted "any embarrassment or anguish caused to Ms. McTeer and her family by the misrepresentations found in the press release." He also stated that: "I have now spoken at length with Ms. McTeer and am in a position to state categorically that as a Roman Catholic, Ms McTeer does not favour abortion, would not consider it for herself nor counsel it for others." Ms. McTeer did not succeed in winning the seat, but the abortion issue does not appear to have been decisive in the result, since her party fared poorly in the whole Ottawa area.

I have given both Ms. McTeer and Bishop Belisle an opportunity to comment. The outline of the events is found in the Ottawa *Citizen*, 19 Nov. 1988, A1, 22 Nov. 1988, B12, and 3 Dec. 1988, D21.

8 *The Canadian Register*, 15 Oct. 1966, 6.

9 *Love Kindness! The Social Teaching of the Canadian Catholic Bishops (1958–1989): A Second Collection*, ed. E.F. Sheridan, S.J., Éditions Paulines and the Jesuit Centre for Social Faith and Justice, 1991, 299 (Submission to the Committee on Pornography and Prostitution Appointed by the Minister of Justice).

10 *Supra* note 8, *ibid.*

11 *Supra* note 8, *ibid.*

12 Report of the Committee on Homosexual Offences and Prostitution, Cmnd. 247, Her Majesty's Stationery Office, 1957, 9–10, par. 13.

13 *Ibid.*, 10, par. 14. The Report was strongly supported by Professor H.L.A. Hart, *Law, Liberty and Morality*, Oxford University Press, 1963, and roundly opposed by Lord Patrick Devlin, *The Enforcement of Morality*, Oxford University Press, 1965.

14 Report of the Episcopal Committee of the C.C.C. on Theory and Policy Concerning Proposed Legislative Changes with Respect to Contraception Information and Sales, Divorce and Abortion, 1966, 16. I have a personal copy since I was a consultant to the Committee, but to the best of my knowledge this document, though apparently intended for the laity, was not generally published. However, it is in complete accord with the fully published statements of the Canadian bishops and therefore seems a valid source to round out episcopal thinking on the Wolfenden Report, since the same conclusion must in any event be implicitly drawn from their other documents.

15 *Supra* note 14, 15.

16 Toronto *Globe and Mail*, 13 Jan. 1968, 29. The Irish bishops on the other hand, recently took the position that the repeal of Ireland's criminalization of homosexuality would damage the status of the family: *The Tablet*, 26 June 1993, 829. The Irish Government introduced the amendment after the European Court of Human Rights

ruled that existing Irish laws against homosexuals violated human rights, particularly the right to privacy.

17 The Conference is quoted to this effect in the Toronto *Star*, 3 Dec. 1986, A18. This 1986 opposition to the prohibition of discrimination against homosexuals considerably affects the credibility of the 1994 episcopal instructions on further Ontario legislation recognizing homosexual relationships as conjugal ones by the Archbishop of Toronto (Toronto *Globe and Mail*, 30 May 1994, A3) and the Archbishop of Ottawa (Ottawa *Citizen*, 2 June 1994, A4).

18 In *Caldwell* v. *Stuart*, [1984] 2 S.C.R. 603, the Supreme Court of Canada found that the employment requirement of religious conformity in a Catholic school system was reasonably necessary to assure the accomplishment of Church objectives in operating Catholic schools, and so was a bona fide qualification for employment under the British Columbia Human Rights Code. Of course, there is a loss of freedom of choice by employers, landlords, etc. under human rights legislation, but it is for the common good. See, e.g., Stephen L. Carter, "Stuck with a Satanist? Religious Autonomy in a Regulated Society," *Commonweal*, 13 Aug. 1993, 15. But this problem extends to any characteristic found objectionable by an employer, etc., and is not limited to homosexuality. In any event, personal distaste is no ground for validly objecting to human rights legislation. It is precisely because of such feelings of distaste that human rights protections are necessary. The Ontario bishops, had, of course, more serious objections, but I believe their fears to be unwarranted in the light of *Caldwell*.

19 Toronto *Star*, 4 Dec. 1986, A8.

20 *Supra* note 9, 83 (Brief to the Minister of Justice on the Family Law Report of the Law Reform Commission of Canada). But in a 1985 statement the bishops said (106): "Measures that

strengthen family values should have priority for the government, whereas measures that will facilitate the dissolution of marriage are of less importance (Brief to the House of Commons Committee on Justice on Bill C-47: An Act Respecting Divorce)."

21 The Canadian Register, 15 Apr. 1967, 16.

22 *Supra* note 9, 183 (Ethical Reflections on Respect for Life, 1983). This position anticipates the Vatican position of 1994: in a Reuters news story entitled "Pope Attacks UN over population conference," Ottawa *Citizen*, 30 April 1994, C 4, it is stated "Pope John Paul has launched an all-out battle over a planned population conference [in Cairo] that the Vatican fears will promote unrestricted abortion and contraception."

23 *Supra* note 9, 183.

24 *Supra* note 9, 225–6 (Submission to the Parliamentary Commission on Abortion).

25 *Supra* note 9, 221.

26 "Religious Belief and Public Morality: A Catholic Governor's Perspective," excerpted in the New York *Times*, 14 Sept. 1984, A21.

27 *Supra* note 26.

28 Encyclical Letter *Centesimus Annus*, Éditions Paulines, 1991, n. 46 at 83.

29 *Supra* note 28, n. 47 at 84.

CHAPTER 5

1 *The Politics of Aristotle*, tr. with notes by Sir Ernest Barker, The Clarendon Press, 1948, III, c. 7, at 132. Having stated the distinction of constitutions on the basis of number, Aristotle immediately transforms it into a distinction based on social class: III, c. 8. The word *politeia* which Aristotle here uses in a restricted sense, translated by Barker in this context as "polity," is actually the same word he uses for a constitution itself. *Politeia, politeuma*

(civic body) and *politikos* (statesmen) are all derivatives of *polis* or city-state.

2 *Supra* note, 1 447: about 40,000 were citizens out of a population of 150,000 to 170,000.

3 *Supra* note 1, IV, c. 8, 207.

4 *The Theory of the Mixed Constitution in Antiquity: A Critical Analysis of Polybius' Political Ideas*, Columbia University Press, 1954, vi. for both quotations.

5 *Supra* note 1, III, c. 15, 165 and 167.

6 *Supra* note 1, III, c. 17, 177.

7 My Ph. D. thesis at the University of Toronto (1957, unpublished) was entitled The Best Form of Government in the Philosophy of St. Thomas Aquinas.

8 *Summa theologiae*, Commissio Parma, 1953, I–II, 95, a. 4.

9 *Supra* note 8, I–II, q. 105, a. 1.

10 *The Dominican Order and Convocation*, Oxford University Press, 1913. The Master General of the Dominicans claimed some years ago that Thomas Jefferson consulted the constitution of the Order "prior to writing the U.S. Constitution" [presumably the Declaration of Independence, since that is what Jefferson wrote]: *National Catholic Reporter*, 16 Jan. 1976, 15.

11 For instance, James A. Weisheipl, *Friar Thomas d'Aquino*, Doubleday, 1974, 146–7, lists some of the provincial chapters St. Thomas attended as preacher general.

12 J. Moss Ives, "St. Thomas Aquinas and the Constitution" (1937), 13 *Thought* 567, 568.

13 *Natural Law: An Introduction to Legal Philosophy*, Hutchinson's University Library, 1951, 11. Professor John Finnis, *Natural Law and Natural Rights*, Clarendon Press, 1980, 221, takes a more nuanced position: "the modern usage of claims of right as the principal counter in political discussion should be recognized ... as a valuable addition to the received vocabu-lary of practical reasonableness (i.e. to the tradition of 'natural law doctrine')."

14 *Reflection on Government*, Oxford University Press, 1942, 36.

15 *Ibid.*, 67–8.

16 E.E.Y. Hales, *The Catholic Church in the Modern World: A Survey from the French Revolution to the Present*, Image Books, 1960, 155.

17 *The Federalist*, ed. E. M. Earle, National Home Library Foundation, No. 51 at 337.

18 My account is drawn mostly from Hales, *supra* note 16, 34–50.

19 Greater amplification of this view will be found in Conor Cruise O'Brien, *The Great Melody: A Thematic Biography and Commented Anthology of Edmund Burke*, University of Chicago Press, 1992.

CHAPTER 6

1 E.E.Y. Hales, *The Catholic Church in the Modern World: A Survey from the French Revolution to the Present*, Image Books ed., 1960, 80. I have drawn generally on this Hales book as a background source.

2 *Supra* note 1, 118.

3 Hales, *supra* note 1, 236, notes of one such secularist: "By September 1904 Combes was in a position to boast, in a speech at Auxerre, that he had closed 13,904 schools."

4 For instance, in respect of France, Leo XIII in 1892 and Pius XI in 1926 both urged Catholics to eschew the errors of the French right. Pius VI also sent a directive to French clergy in 1796 to accept the authority of the government, but unfortunately it was never published. See Hales, *supra* note 1, 47–8, 234–5 and 240.

5 Hales, *supra* note 1, 173.

6 "Religious Freedom," 672–4, in *The Documents of Vatican II*, ed. Walter M. Abbott, S.J., Guild Press, 1966, 673.

7 *Supra* note 1, 93.

8 Both quotations are from John Nurser, *The Reign of Conscience: Individual, Church and State in Lord Acton's History of Liberty*, Garland Publishing, Inc., 1987, 94–5 and 80. Acton was more a teacher than a writer. He wrote little and his views have had to be compiled in part from his notes. Yet, because of his position as Regius Professor of History at Cambridge and as director of the Cambridge Modern History Project, his influence on other thinkers has been enormous. In our own day, Canada's Prime Minister Trudeau, for example, frequently cited Acton.

9 Conor Cruise O'Brien, *The Great Melody: A Thematic Biography and Commented Anthology of Edmund Burke*, University of Chicago Press, 1992, 92.

10 *Supra* note 1, 153.

11 "The Constitution's Protection of Individual Rights: The Real Role of the Religion Clauses" (1988), 49 *Univ. Pitts. L. Rev.* 717, 718.

12 *Supra* note 8, 51.

13 *Supra* note 8, 99.

14 *Supra* note 8, 105–6.

15 *Supra* note 8, 61.

16 I have based my summary of Maritain's views on his most mature work in this area, *Man and the State*, University of Chicago Press, 1951. This quotation is at 108.

17 *Supra* note 16, 108.

18 Reprinted in the New York *Times*, 16 Sept. 1984, 24E.

19 *Supra* note 6, 673.

20 *Supra* note 6, n. 2 at 678–9.

21 *Supra* note 6, n. 2 at 679.

22 *Supra* note 6, n. 6 at 684–5.

23 *Supra* note 6, n. 7 at 687.

24 *Supra* note 6, n. 6 at 685.

25 *Supra* note 6, 674.

26 *Supra* note 6, 673.

27 *Supra* note 6, 673. Brian Mullady, O.P., "Religious Freedom" (1994), 58 *The Thomist* 93, has recently attempted a rehabilitation of the *Syllabus of Errors*: He concludes (108):

> "[T]he *Syllabus of Errors* and *Dignitatis Humanae* [i.e., the *Declaration on Religious Freedom*] are in perfect theoretical accord on the nature of religious freedom. The former emphasizes the intellect as bound to seek the truth, the latter the will in its freedom from exterior coercion to be a natural, human act. The fact that they represent different juridical ideas about the state religion is due only to the application of these principles in various times ... The only intelligent conclusion is that there is a homogeneous and not a heterogeneous development of doctrine exhibited by the two documents."

28 *An Essay on the Development of Christian Doctrine*, Longmans Green, 1909, 35.

29 *Supra* note 28, 38.

30 *Supra* note 28, 39.

CHAPTER 7

1 The Master of the Rolls in England, the Rt. Hon. Sir Thomas Bingham, has recently presented a legal argument in favour of Britain's acceptance of the European Convention as part of its own domestic law: "The European Convention on Human Rights: Time to Incorporate" (1993), 109 *L.Q.R.* 390.

2 *Palko* v. *Connecticut*, 302 U.S. 319, 327 (1937).

3 At an early stage of Congressional consideration, under Madison's influence the proposed First Amendment read in the Senate: "Congress shall

make no law establishing religion, or prohibiting the free exercise thereof, *nor shall the rights of conscience be infringed*" (emphasis mine). See Joseph M. Lynch, "Madison's Religion Proposals Judicially Confounded: A Study in the Constitutional Law of Conscience" (1990), 20 *Seton Hall L. Rev.* 418, 428.

4 [1985] 1 S.C.R. 295, 345–6. Dickson C.J.C. was only Dickson J. at the time the case was argued, but was elevated to the chief justiceship shortly thereafter, and well before the decision was rendered. An interesting case on freedom of conscience and religion in the Court was *Jones* v. The *Queen* [1986], 2 S.C.R. 284, in which the Court held that the Alberta compulsory education law did not offend the Charter (Wilson J. dissenting).

5 In fact, he says as much in the passage I cite, *infra* note 8, from *Big M Drug Mart:* "Equally protected [as religious beliefs and practice] and for the same reasons are expressions and manifestations of religious non-belief and refusals to participate in religious practice."

6 *R.* v. *Morgentaler* [1988], 1 S.C.R. 30, 177–9.

7 Encyclical Letter *Centesimus Annus*, Éditions Paulines, 1991, n. 29 at 53.

8 *Supra* note 4, 346–7.

9 Linden J.A. recently wrote for the Federal Court of Appeal in *Roach* v. *Canada* (1994), 164 N.R. 370, 379:

It seems ... that freedom of conscience is broader than freedom of religion. The latter relates more to religious views derived from established religious institutions, whereas the former is aimed at protecting views based on strongly held moral ideas of right and wrong, not necessarily founded on any organized religious principles.

10 *Snyder* v. *Massachusetts*, 291 U.S. 97, 105 (1934). *Snyder* was cited by Goldberg J., Warren C.J. and Brennan J. in their joint opinion in *Griswold* v. *Connecticut*, 381 U.S. 479 (1965).

11 *Planned Parenthood of South-Eastern Pennsylvania* v. *Casey*, 112 S. Ct. 2791, 2806 (1992). In the same case Blackmun J., wrote (2846):

"Because motherhood has a dramatic impact on a woman's educational prospects, employment opportunities, and self-determination, restrictive abortion laws deprive her of control over her life."

For these reasons, for him "the decision whether or not to beget or bear a child" lies at "the very heart of this cluster of constitutionally protected choices."

12 Josef Pieper, *Prudence*, Pantheon Books, 1959, 17–19. Pieper's small books on prudence, justice, and fortitude and temperance are generally considered twentieth-century classics in the Thomistic tradition.

13 *Supra* note 12, 13.

14 *Veritatis Splendor*, Éditions Paulines, 1993, n. 32 at 53.

15 *Supra* note 12, 55.

16 As I quoted the principle from the *Declaration*, *supra* in chapter 6, it read: "in matters religious no one is to be forced to act in a manner contrary to his own beliefs" (emphasis added). Since I have applied to conscience in particular what is there said of "matters religious" generally, I here add for the sake of clarification the words "of a personal nature," which describe the realm of conscience as a principled basis of ethical life.

17 319 U.S. 624 (1943). Actually, Justice Jackson did not refer to conscience, and his opinion appears to waver as to whether what was infringed was the free exercise of religion or free speech.

18 *The Documents of Vatican II*, ed. Walter M. Abbott, S.J., Guild Press, 1966, n. 2 at 679.

19 *Supra* note 7, n. 47 at 85.

20 110 S. Ct. 1595 (1990).

21 Stephen L. Carter, "The Resurrection of Religious Freedom?", The Supreme Court — Comment (1993), 107 *Harv. L. Rev.* 118.

22 113 S. Ct. 2217 (1993). The quotation from Blackmun J. is at 2250, quoting from his own dissent in *Smith*, at 1615.

23 113 S. Ct. 2141 (1993).

24 *Supra* note 21, 140.

25 Harry W. Wellington, *Interpreting the Constitution: The Supreme Court and the Process of Adjudication,* Yale University Press, 1990, 116.

26 At least this is true in Canada, where abortions are performed routinely until the twentieth week, and from the twentieth to the twenty-fourth week only where there is serious congenital abnormality. Any later abortions are frequently transmitted to the United States, where abortions are carried out for serious congenital abnormalities up to the thirty-second week.

27 L.W. Sumner, *Abortion and Moral Theory,* Princeton University Press, 1981, 150.

28 *Ibid.,* 155.

29 *Ibid.,* 155–6. Prime Minister Trudeau's original reasoning in support of the 1969 decriminalization of therapeutic abortion was based on the mother's right of self-defence.

30 *Ibid.,* 154.

31 The U.S. Supreme Court held in *Planned Parenthood* v. *Ashcroft*, 462 U.S. 476 (1983) and *Thornburgh* v. *American College of Obstetricians and Gynaecologists*, 476 U.S. 747 (1986) that the law may not force a physician to make a trade-off between a woman's health and additional percentage points of fetal survival, but that it may require safeguards like the presence of a second physician.

32 Judith Jarvis Thomson, "A Defense of Abortion" (1971), 1 *Phil. & Pub. Affairs* 47, 66. The article is reprinted in *The Rights and Wrongs of Abortion: A Philosophy & Public Affairs Reader,* ed. by Marshall Cohen, Thomas Nagel and Thomas Scanlon, Princeton University Press, 1974.

33 *Mallette* v. *Shulman* (1990), 72 O.R. (2d) 417, 424. The right of an adult Jehovah's Witness to reject blood transfusions was extended in a recent decision by the New Brunswick Court of Appeal to a 15-year-old boy afflicted with leukemia: *Globe and Mail*, 26 Ap. 1994, A6 (Joshua Walker case).

34 *Ibid.,* 426.

35 *Re Wintersgill* (1981), 131 D.L.R. (3d) 184; See Bernard M. Dickens, "The Modern Function and Limits of Parental Rights" (1981), 97 *L.Q.R.* 462. This view is impliedly also supported by the Supreme Court of Canada in *Hopp* v. *Lepp* [1980], 2 S.C.R. 192 and *Reibl* v. *Hughes* [1980], 2 S.C.R. 880, by the British Columbia Court of Appeal in *Young* v. *Young* (1990), 75 D.L.R. (4th) 46 and by the Supreme Court again in *Young* on further appeal.

36 *Re McTavish* (1986), 32 D.L.R. (4th) 394; *Re B.* (1982), 2 C.R.R. 329; *Pentland* v. *Pentland* (1978), 86 D.L.R. (3d) 585; *Forsyth* v. *Children's Aid Society of Kingston and County of Frontenac* (1962), 35 D.L.R. (2d) 690 (but the order of temporary wardship in the local Children's Aid Society was quashed because of a violation of natural justice).

CHAPTER 8

1 "Religion, Science and Pluralism: The Catholic Politician and Abortion" (1985), 3 *Can. Cath. Rev.* 52. Professor Jacques Croteau, "Le foetus humain, une personne? Essai philosophique" (1989), 20 *R.G.D.* 513

argues that the legal notion of a person should have the same extension as the ontological notion, but this, it seems to me, is for the law and not for philosophy to decide. In *Tremblay* v. *Daigle* [1989], 2 S.C.R. 530, 567, the Supreme Court of Canada seemed to accept that this was not the tradition of the common law, when it said "Anglo-Canadian Courts ... have consistently reached the conclusion that to enjoy rights, a foetus must be born alive." In *Roe* v. *Wade*, 410 U.S. 113, 156–7 (1973) the United States Supreme Court rejected the argument that the fetus is a person within the meaning of the Fourteenth Amendment, and concluded that the word "person" has application only postnatally.

2 "Saint Augustine: Christianity in a Pluralistic Culture" (1987), 5 *Can. Cath. Rev.* 214, 218.

3 Encyclical Letter *Centesimus Annus*, Éditions Paulines, 1991, n. 46 at 82.

4 Encyclical Letter *Pacem in Terris*, America Press, 1963, n. 25 at 9.

5 A monumental, though unfinished, study of democracy in the Thomistic tradition by Mortimer Adler and Walter Farrell, O.P., laid a groundwork for the theory that democracy is the only fully moral form of government, since it is the only form that gives full scope and reality to the principle of consent: "The Theory of Democracy" (1941), 3 *The Thomist* 397, 588; (1942), 4 *The Thomist* 121, 286, 446 and 692; (1943), 6 *The Thomist* 49, 251 and 367; (1944), 7 *The Thomist* 80.

6 Both quotations are taken from his address "Religious Belief and Public Morality: A Catholic Governor's Perspective," New York *Times*, 14 Sept. 1984, A21.

7 Abortion in Ireland has always been forbidden, a position which was bolstered by an amendment to the Irish Constitution in 1983, requiring the state to take active steps against abortion, but in a case involving a four-teen-year-old who said she had been raped, the Supreme Court of Ireland voted 4 to 1 to permit her to travel to London to obtain an abortion (the Attorney General having forbidden her to travel for that purpose). Finlay C.J., as excerpted in the New York *Times*, 6 March 1992, A8, said for the majority:

> "I therefore conclude that the proper test to be applied is that if it is established as a matter of probability that there is a real and substantial risk to the life — as distinct from the health — of the mother, which can only be avoided by the termination of her pregnancy, that such termination is permissible, having regard to the true interpretation of Article 40.3.3 of the Constitution."

In June 1993 the Irish Parliament, rejecting pleas from Catholic Bishops, passed a law removing age limits on the sale of condoms by the device of excluding them from the legislative definition of contraceptives. See also Ruth L. O'Halloran, "How Catholic are the Irish?," *Commonweal*, 11 Mar. 1994, 7, who suggests that Ireland may be becoming less Catholic but more christian.

CHAPTER 9

1 One such protester who refused to give her name was jailed on a contempt charge by a judge who decided that he could not conduct a trial without knowing the name of the defendant; she was released after 14 months when her identity was discovered by police investigation: New York *Times*, 12 May 1994, A13. The U.S. has now passed legislation making blockades of abortion clinics a federal crime: New York *Times*, 13 May 1994, A1. A few days earlier a Texas jury in a civil suit ordered anti-abortion protesters to pay $1 million in punitive damages for conspiring to disrupt abortion clinics during the 1992 Republican National

Convention: Toronto *Globe and Mail*, 10 May 1994, A10.

2 "Democracy and Civil Disobedience" (1971), 49 *Can. Bar Rev.* 222, 278–9. I have drawn freely upon this article in the foregoing analysis.

3 Lisa Sowle Cahill, "Abortion, Sex and Gender: The Church's Public Voice," *America*, 22 May 1993, 6, 11.

4 Lynn D. Wardle, "Protecting The Rights of Conscience of Health Care Providers" (1993), 14 J. of *Legal Medicine* 177, 178.

5 [1985] 1 S.C.R. 295, 336–7. See also *R.* v. *Edwards Books and Arts Limited* [1986], 2 S.C.R. 713.

6 Toronto *Globe and Mail*, 31 August 1994, A1. In *Madsen* v. *Women's Health Center* a majority of the U.S. Supreme Court upheld a state court injunction establishing such a buffer zone: New York *Times*, 1 July 1994, A16. The United States Congress has also passed a Freedom of Access to Clinic Entrances Act, which makes it a crime to obstruct an abortion clinic or to interfere with patients or staff.

CHAPTER 10

1 Such an approach is well developed by Germain Grisez and Joseph M. Boyle Jr., *Life and Death with Liberty and Justice: A Contribution to the Euthanasia Debate*, University of Notre Dame Press, 1979.

2 The full text was carried in *L'Osservatore Romano*, 30 June 1980. I have quoted from a pamphlet, *Euthanasia: Recent Declarations of Popes and Bishops*, Life Ethics Centre, 1983.

3 *Ibid.,* 7.

4 *Ibid.,* 16.

5 *Ibid.,* 17.

6 Fr. Richard A. McCormick, S.J., and Robert Veatch, Note, "The Preservation of Life and Self-

Determination" (1980), 41 *Theological Studies* 390, 395, argue that in such a case "the family is normally in the best position to judge the real interests of the incompetent patient."

7 247 U.S. 200, (1927). In *E. (Mrs.)* v. *E.* [1986], 2 S.C.R. 388, the Supreme Court of Canada held that involuntary non-therapeutic sterilization is a serious intrusion on the basic rights of an individual person.

8 *Le Monde*, 21 Aug. 1993, 8.

9 *Euthanasia: Recent Declarations of Popes and Bishops, supra* note 2, 13.

10 Toronto *Globe and Mail*, 25 Aug. 1993, A1; the Montreal *Gazette*, 25 Aug. 1993, B1.

11 Euthanasia, Aiding Suicide and Cessation of Treatment, Report 20, Law Reform Commission of Canada, 1983, 18.

12 111 L. Ed. 2d 224 (1990). The opinion of the Court was delivered by Rehnquist C.J., joined by White, O'Connor, Scalia and Kennedy JJ. Brennan J. joined by Marshall and Blackmun JJ., wrote one dissent, Stevens J. another. The decision of the State Supreme Court is found at 760 S.W. 2d 408 (1988). The quotation from that Court is at 426.

13 *Supra* note 12, 273. The citation for the New Jersey case is *In re Jobes*, 108 NJ 394, 416, 529 A2d 434, 445 (1987).

14 *Supra* note 12, 255.

15 *Airedale NHS Trust* v. *Bland* [1993], 1 All E.R. 821, 866.

16 *Ibid.,* 866.

17 *Ibid.,* 867.

18 *Ibid.,* 870–1.

19 *Rodriguez* v. *British Columbia (Attorney General)* [1993], 3 W.W.R. 553.

20 (1994), 158 N.R. 1. Two other sections of the Charter were also in play in Rodriguez: s. 12 (cruel and unusual

punishment) and s. 15 (equality). But as neither of these sections was dealt with by all of the judges who wrote, I have felt free to omit them from discussion for purposes of simplification.

21 *Ibid.*, 32. John Paul II was apparently pleased with the majority decision, though he tactfully praised, not the Court, but the Canadian bishops for opposing Sue Rodriguez's search for legal relief: Ottawa *Citizen*, 20 Nov. 1993, A3. The Pontiff reportedly warned that "legalization of assisted suicide was an offence to human dignity and opened the way to totalitarianism."

22 *Ibid.*, 37. The Court also drew attention to the fact that the official position of all relevant medical associations is against decriminalizing assisted suicide. Hollinrake J.A. in the British Columbia Court of Appeal, *supra* note 19, 582, enumerated the Associations as follows: "The Canadian Medical Association, the British Medical Association and the World Medical Association all condemn the practice of active euthanasia and physician assisted suicide."

23 The Court cites *Nancy B.* v. *Hôtel Dieu de Québec* (1992), 86 D.L.R. (4th) 385 (Que. S.C.), *Mallette* v. *Shulman* (1990), 72 O.R. (2d) 417 (C.A.), and *Cruzan* v. *Director Missouri Health Department* (1990), 111 L. Ed. 2d. 224.

24 [1988] 1 S.C.R. 30.

25 *Supra* note 20, 52.

26 *Supra* note 20, 56.

27 *Supra* note 20, 59.

28 *Supra* note 20, 66.

29 *Supra* note 20, 127.

30 House of Lords, Report of the Select Committee on Medical Ethics, Vol. I — Report (HL Paper 21-I), London: Her Majesty's Stationery Office, ordered to be printed 31 January 1994. The 14-member committee was chaired by Lord Walton of Detchant. In a sense the problem is seen as a

more acute one in the United Kingdom, because assisted suicide is there charged as murder, carrying a mandatory minimum life sentence on conviction, rather than under a lesser provision, such as s. 241 of the Canadian Code. The Walton Committee strongly endorsed the recommendation that the mandatory life sentence for murder should be abolished (53–4).

31 *Ibid.*, 48.

32 *Ibid.*, 49.

33 *Ibid.*, 57.

34 *Nancy B.* v. *Hôtel Dieu de Québec*, *supra* note 23.

35 Toronto *Globe and Mail*, 30 May 1994, A19. The unanimous report of the 24-member advisory group was released on 25 May 1994.

36 I do not analogize the feeding tube to the disconnection of the respirator in *In Re Quinlan*, 70 N.J. 10, 355 A 2d 647, (1976), because the former, as I understand it, is a simple tube dispensing food in liquid form, the latter a more technologically complex device. In my criticism of the reasoning and result in *Bland*, I am somewhat on the same wave length as J.M. Finnis, "*Bland*: Crossing the Rubicon?", Note (1993), 109 L.Q.R. 329, 333, who writes:

> "What is misshapen and indefensible is a law that treats as criminal a harmful 'act' while treating as lawful (and indeed compulsory) an 'omission,' with the very *same intent*, by one who has a duty to care for the person injured."

Professor Finnis picks up the word "misshapen" from Lord Mustill in *Bland* who, even though concurring with Lord Goff, described the "legal structure" on which the decision was based as "morally and intellectually misshapen": *supra* note 15, 885. Karen Ann Quinlan, by the way, lived from 1976 until 1985 after the removal of the respirator, and her brain is still being studied by PVS specialists: Toronto *Globe and Mail*, 4 June 1994, D8.

37 *Supra* note 30, 52.

CHAPTER 11

1 A.D. Sertillanges, O.P., *Foundations of Thomistic Philosophy*, 1931, trans. Godfrey Anstruther, O.P., Sands, 234.

2 "Positive Law and the Moral Law" (1961), 2 Current Law and Social Problems 89, 94–5. My analysis here is largely based upon that article and my article, "St. Thomas and Legal Obligation" (1961), 35 *The New Scholasticism* 281.

3 *Ibid.*, 103–4.

4 "Law, Morals and Positivism" (1961), 14 *Univ. Toronto Law Journal* 1, 26.

5 347 U.S. 483 (1954).

6 Valerie Kerruish, *Jurisprudence as Ideology*, Routledge, 1991, 3–4.

7 Psalm 115: 4–8, *The Psalms: A New Translation*, The Grail (England), 1963.

8 *Love Kindness! The Social Teaching of the Canadian Catholic Bishops (1958–1989): A Second Collection*, ed. by E.F. Sheridan, S.J., Éditions Paulines and the Jesuit Centre for Social Faith and Justice, 1991, 221 (from the 1990 Submission to the Parliamentary Committee on Abortion).

CHAPTER 12

1 *Democracy and Dissent: A Theory of Judicial Review*, Harvard University Press, 1980, 181. He locates something like this approach in much of the work of the Warren Court, which in his view was foreshadowed by Chief Justice Stone's famous footnote in *United States* v. *Carolene Products Co.*, 304 U.S. 144, 152–3, n. 4 (1938).

2 *Ibid.*, 87.

3 "Validation: A Moral Concept" (1968), 5 *ARSP* 143, 150.

4 Both quotations are from "The Complacent Democracies," *The New York Review of Books*, 15 July 1993, 17. John Garvey, "Democracy & Its Limits: It's Wonderful; It's Not Enough," *Commonweal*, 13 Aug. 1993, 9, comments favourably on the Pfaff thesis.

5 On the question of democratic leadership, see Gary Wills, *Certain Trumpets: The Call of Leaders*, Simon & Schuster, 1994.

6 "Unity in the Secular City" in *One Church, Two Nations?*, ed. Le Blanc and Edinborough, Longmans, 1968, 146, 147.

7 *The Documents of Vatican II*, ed. Walter M. Abbott, S.J., Guild Press, 1966, n. 43 at 243.

8 *Ibid.*, Decree on the Apostolate of the Laity, n. 7 at 498.

9 *Ibid.*, n. 31 at 57.

10 *The Secular City*, New York, 1965.

11 *Supra* note 7, n. 43 at 243.

12 National hierarchies have begun to assert themselves in this area. If they go beyond the setting forth of abstract principles they should expect to find themselves in the same hurly-burly with other social and political commentators. Certainly the episcopate's practical admonitions cannot relieve the laity of their own responsibilities in this domain.

13 This is Thomistic moral teaching: see my article, "St. Thomas and Legal Obligation" (1961), 35 *The New Scholasticism* 281. At a deeper level a distinction made by the Canadian bishops between law as precept and law as the dynamic structure of personal being is helpful: *Love Kindness! The Social Teaching of the Canadian Catholic Bishops (1958–1989): A Second Collection*, ed. by E.F. Sheridan, S.J., Éditions Paulines and the Jesuit Centre for Social Faith and

Justice, 1991, 171 ff. (Statement on
the Formation of Conscience, 1973).
All forms of preceptive law are open
and subject to the freedom of the children of God in His Spirit, a fact which
the bishops say "establishes the ultimate priority of personal conscience
informed by the Spirit of Christ in the
case of possible conflict with extrinsic
law" (172).

14 *Supra* note 7, n. 7 at 498.

15 *Supra* note 7, n. 43 at 243.

16 *Pacem in Terris*, America Press, 1963,
n. 158 at 50.

17 "Democracy and the Social System,"
*Internal War: Problems and
Approaches*, ed. Harry Eckstein, Free
Press of Glencoe, 1964, 267 ff.

18 "The Open Society and The Open
Church and Synagogue" (1974), 69
Religious Education 124.

19 *Supra* note 5, 155.

20 See *Re An Act to Amend the Education
Act (Ontario)* [1987], 1 S.C.R. 1148.

21 A good example of the need for
actions not to await theology occurred
in the work of marriage tribunals.
These tribunals could not wait for the
new Code of Canon Law in 1983 to
begin applying the relevant principles
of Vatican II and *Humanae Vitae*, and
their decisions were accordingly far in
advance of the theological synthesis of
marriage.

22 Éditions Paulines, 1993, n. 106 at 157.

23 *Ibid.,* n. 107 at 158.

INDEX
TO NAMES AND CASES

WIDENER UNIVERSITY
WOLFGRAM
LIBRARY
CHESTER, PA